Say the Name

The author lighting a memorial
candle in Ravensbrück in 1995.

# Say the Name

## A SURVIVOR'S TALE
### IN PROSE AND POETRY

*Judith H. Sherman*

University of New Mexico Press
Albuquerque

15  14  13  12  11          4  5  6  7  8

PAPERBOUND ISBN-13: 978-0-8263-3432-9

Library of Congress Cataloging-in-Publication Data

Sherman, Judith H.
  Say the name : a survivor's tale in prose and poetry /
Judith H. Sherman.
      p. cm.
    ISBN 0-8263-3431-8 (CLOTH : ALK. PAPER) —
    ISBN 0-8263-3432-6 (PBK. : ALK. PAPER)
  1. Sherman, Judith H.—Childhood and youth.
  2. Jews—Slovakia—Kurima—Biography.
  3. Jewish children in the Holocaust—Biography.
  4. Concentration camp inmates—Germany—Biography.
  5. Holocaust, Jewish (1939–1945)—Slovakia—Kurima—
    Personal narratives.
  6. Ravensbrück (Concentration camp)
  7. Holocaust, Jewish (1939–1945)—Poetry.
  8. Kurima (Slovakia)—Biography. I. Title.
    DS135.S55S55    2005
    940.53'18'092—dc22

                              2005000961

Book design and composition by Damien Shay

Body type is Minion 10.5/14
Display is Caflisch Script and Impact

*To David Carrasco*
*You give ear to my silence*

❦

# Contents

# Foreword

BY DAVÍD CARRASCO

**Apell.** Roll call. The wake up siren sounds at
four a.m.—the sound of dread and ugliness. To
help me get up I have developed a system that
works for me, "resistance," I call it, and get up.
Family injunction in operation. The other
option to getting up is being beaten to death,
thrown into a punishment bunker, bullets—but
"resistance" works for me—a gift to the family,
a gift from the family.

— Judith Sherman, *Say the Name*

Judith Sherman got up from her years of memories, nightmares,
private resistance, and public silence to write *Say the Name*, this
book about her childhood, her imprisonment in Ravensbrück
death camp, and her "liberation." She tells us she was armed by
the "family injunction," a promise the family members made to
each other "to survive/to live" as they were being sucked into what
she calls the "primal night" of the Holocaust! She survived and now,
thanks to her skilled poetry and prose, her story survives. The
chronological backbone of this book tells of her childhood home
in Kurima, Czechoslovakia, several deportations, hiding in homes
and in the forest, her struggles in several prisons including a converted castle, undergoing torture and witnessing murder in

Ravensbrück, and her liberation. Along the way we meet and grow to care about and mourn for many individuals, especially women, whom she encounters, remembers, and now gives us their names. The book ends in the present day with her reflections on the destruction of families in the 9/11 attacks and on her own legacy for her children. As readers will experience, this book is an expression of Judith's ongoing *resistance* to Hitler and the Holocaust, and it is a gift to her family and to all *our* families.

The narrative, in prose and poems, speaks with two voices—the thirteen-to-fourteen-year-old girl who experienced the dismemberment of family, European Jewry, and perhaps even God; and in the voice of the adult survivor remembering family and friends, raging against rape and murder, writing poems, and searching for a dialogue with a God who wasn't there. Here are a few examples of both of those voices, sometimes intermingling as she writes about the simple things that both children and God's followers might care about when facing disaster,

> I am not yet fourteen. I think of home. I would like to be
> with my mother. I never am any more. So much to tell her.
> All bundles are to be left on the side... The contents, flash-
> light, sweater, photographs, sewing kit, instant coffee, a mug,
> perhaps a prayer book, a book, brush, house keys, socks—
> will be integrated into the camp economy, or more likely the
> German Reich. But not the connections. They are severed...

and

> I shall never not value shoes,
> life is from the ground up,
> life with shoes, perhaps,
> without-death...

and later,

Come Messiah
Is not the apocalypse
Your cue
To do
The Messiah thing?

Tragically, the Messiah was not on cue and Sherman writes her life story with lamentation from what she calls "survivorship territory" where she "lives on two tracks always,"—the Holocaust track and the track of life today. Selecting fruit at the grocery store, taking a shower, and seeing railroad tracks "trigger" her memories of "the selection," "gas chambers," and "transports" to death camps, and she realizes she will always be both old and young at the same time.

I am old in this late year
But my soul — my soul
Is peopled with parents
Who are younger than my children
My brother will forever be nine.

While this Holocaust story might be read as a gripping example of women's testimonial literature, it is important to emphasize that Sherman has written this book to *testify*, and sometimes we have the impression she is both a witness for the victims and the inquisitor of God in the courtroom of the Shoah. She stands up and gives evidence before us and her God of the relentless sufferings caused by the "experts in humiliation," at camps where the "whip reclaims the essence of the place—power, superiority, violence." She testifies and shrewdly tries to draw God into her ongoing ordeal and trial as a partner in dialogue. When she doesn't elicit a response, she skillfully rebukes God through a series of poems and pointed questions about his absence when he was most desperately needed. She writes when remembering the women shot dead for trying to aid others,

Are You not tempted,
Lord,
To intervene
Lend a hand
Prevent a scream?

As no response was forthcoming, Sherman is driven to speak up for the others. As though in a courtroom she writes in "Reluctant Witness" that she is here to "testify to their murder of Anna" who starved, Evka who was beaten to death, Daniel who was gassed, Johanna who was shot down . . . leading her to ask three simple yet profound questions,

Where is the judge?
Where are you, judge?
Is there a judge?

Judith Sherman is symbolically standing up for the many who cannot stand up for themselves, and her interrogation of God wakes us up and raises the absurd possibility that there was no judge. No justice or mercy giver! It's not that the judge didn't show up on time, it's that the judge abdicated his role, failed to pay attention, intervene, and produce awe with his justice, his love. She and we are left to wonder if Anyone is out there listening, then or now. Sherman's work is a truly compelling narrative in that it treats both God and humans with "life bestowing awareness." At one point she gives us her definition of God or what he would have to be to live up to his Biblical reputation. It's a simple definition, "Accountability is Divinity," and she's insisting on this accountability for the humans we meet in this book and more.

I remember the morning lecture on the Terror of History when I first met Judith Sherman. I arrived at the Princeton University lecture hall with a feeling of paralysis in the face of lecturing on the religious meaning of the unspeakable cruelties of the Lager. I chastised myself, "What led me to give a single week in the semester's course on the religious dimensions in human experience to the overwhelming story of the Holocaust? Who was I to interpret Elie Wiesel's stunning account, *Night*? I don't have the imagination, words, or knowledge to help students to be attentive to this 'human experience.'" I admitted my crisis of language to the students, that talking about such a monumental horror was too much to handle. Words fail, utterly, in the face of the Holocaust. I said that this failure of language to illuminate reminded me, in a reverse way, of my first white water trip through the Grand Canyon.

In the midst of the mysterious time depth of the Grand Canyon, the stunning sunshine, the breathtaking beauty, the heights of rock walls, oases of the side canyons with flowing springs, we passengers would utter our exclamations like we were describing God or Paradise on Earth—"Amazing," "Awesome," "Astonishing," "Nothing like it in the World," "Unbelievable," "Incredible," "Beautiful beyond Belief," "Overwhelming"—and the second each of these exclamations came out of our mouths they drooped like empty balloons and fell into the depth of the canyon. Well, the Holocaust is the Grand Canyon of Terror and if you've ever seen the Grand Canyon in person or confronted the Holocaust you'll know why words fail. Why silence is an option. Any furious exclamations, roaring condemnations, big words, or strained comparisons that I could offer would just droop like little bits of banal absurdity and sink into the darkness of the Shoah. Think about it! What do these names mean, what synonyms could you rightfully use—Auschwitz, Treblinka, Dachau? Six million gassed and burned! We are driven into silence, into depression, into non-verbal attention. But to be silent in the face of this Grand Canyon of Horror makes even less sense to me.

And so I went on. At the end of the lecture a line of students met me to talk quickly about their individual interests. At the end of the line was Judith Sherman who I had not yet met but who had been sitting in on my course with other senior citizens. She said something like "I've never heard a non-Jew speak the way you did today about the Holocaust and I want to thank you. I am a survivor of the Ravensbrück death camp and I've written this poem which I would like you to read." We talked briefly and I learned that she had, for the most part, remained silent about her experiences. She quickly passed by and I sensed an opening between us. Later that day I read her poem,

> God, that particular pain
> Is too much for me
> You have it and
> Be branded

The terseness of the poem and its challenge to God seized my attention. I called and invited her to speak in the class the following week to tell of her experiences in Ravensbrück, read some of her poetry, and speak of her survival. Reluctantly, but with signs of a deep interest, she agreed. She came and we sat together at a table in front of two hundred students. She spoke haltingly at first; we held hands during some of her talk, and she read some of her poems and used them as openings to describe and interpret her experiences. She told about the first time German soldiers entered her home:

> A gun with a bayonet is pointing at my sleeping head

> A nightmare this — but it is real
> Happening when

I'm not quite ten, and the resulting feelings of TERROR
   and FEAR.

She heard her mother say, "Shoot us or leave us alone." She wept
when she read the poem about her younger brother Karpu being
gassed, how she hoped that someone was there with him at the
horrible end. She spoke of the "miracles" that saved her and the
pain about those not saved. She opened up and opened us up to
her story and to her thoughts about God. Never in my many years
of teaching have I heard a quietness of attention, respect, and awe
fill an auditorium of students like that day, and I've heard some
of the best lecturers in the world. But it wasn't just the story. It was
the woman and her way of telling the story—the story that is in
this book.

   A year later she spoke again in my class, only this time there
were many more pages of prose and poetry. This time we learned
of the forced and brutal instability of her flight in the woods, her
probing of Nazi rationalizations of humiliation and death, of her
withstanding experiments in the camp hospital and of the miracles that saved her there and the horror and shame of the "selection" of others. We heard more of her questions for God, the
embarrassing questions she posed to him. We heard her invite God
to come down Jacob's ladder because "I will not deal with angels.
I'll wait till you arrive" so she could take God's hand and show his
Godly eyes horrors that result in "divine grief."

   She spoke again the following year, and now there were thirty
pages and we heard of her shrinking teenage world made up of
powerless parents, unprotected children, where "fear is normal."
We heard her ask, referring to the Nazi's hunting children down
in the forests, "God, how are we so visible to them and so invisible to You? You owe us visibility."

   When I moved to Harvard she came to speak in my class here,
and now there were chapters! We heard more about her "forms of
resistance" in the face of the grueling, freezing, dangerous hours

standing in line, where she survived by thinking "of every thought I ever had, every place I have ever been to, every person I ever knew." And then in true Judith Sherman style, she thought "up new categories to move time along." And then she invited us to her funeral, "to my un-Auschwitz funeral," telling us that the attire was optional but "no stripes, please." Again God comes in for her critique:

> You come too Lord
> (were you too embarrassed to
> attend in Auschwitz?)
> You come too, Lord
> And smile —
> Your will be done.
> No! Not smile.
> Just be

As readers will discover, there are many such challenges to the Lord in this book. The birth of the Messiah, the red apples of Eden, the sacrifice of Isaac, and even the possible death of God are all scenes she re-imagines. But her purpose is not just an individual search for God in this abyss but to say the names and account for as many of those who "know the finality of the Final Solution."

Her directness and strength, the compactness and playfulness of the cry in her language and her creative and critical inquisitiveness constitute a very distinctive voice in literature about the Holocaust and its family legacies. In the face of the memories of the dead and all that death, Judith affirms life. It is she, not I, who "lets the terror of history terrify." She remembers the branding, requires us to be attentive and never wavers from the knowledge that Auschwitz and Ravensbrück are *part* of her life and legacy. Toward the end of her book she addresses death in the same gritty way she speaks about people and to God. She writes, "Death stand aside/do not hover/by my side" as she leaps "to touch the sun, push children's swings...," and in the fortitude of that spirited fourteen-year-old she outruns the Nazi reaper and tells him, "Don't mess with me/you bloated creep/you cannot/run as fast/as me."

With this book she passes on to her children and the generations to come "a gift to the family, a gift from the family." She gives sound and words to and makes indelible the memories of her (and our) lost ones, and she knows "Connections-Friendships," and "a touch of genesis," and works in her own garden nearby to where she wrote *Say the Name*.

# Acknowledgments

That my story should not have happened, I know. That it should be told is the conviction of Professor Davíd Carrasco of Harvard University. He propels me from silence to voice.

I am fortunate in my strong early connections of family, place and God. I am fortunate in my post-Holocaust connections of family, friends, and God. God to wrestle with—for accountability. Reuven, my husband, transcribes my longhand writing onto the computer and allows the grammatical errors to stand. At all times he manages my deficiencies and revels in my strengths. He is present.

My children, David, Allen, and Ora, you connect me to the gladness of my Kurima family. Your existence fills the present. How lovely you bring your spouses, Gina and Eric, to enhance our family. And grandchildren—Ariel, Ilana, Aaron, Sara, Michael. Allen, you read the narrative as it develops. I lovingly acknowledge your intelligent, pithy, loving comments.

My sister Mirjam shares my story. I feel her presence as I write. Joshua, her son, brings a keen interest to the history and the personal.

Thank you friends for reading, respecting, suggesting and unequivocally supporting: Drs. Adaia and Abe Shumsky, Dov Troy,

Cantor Eli and Lynne Perlman, and Dr. Hans and Ruth Fisher. Thank you Helen Oxenberg, my principal sounding board. Ed Gavurin and his computer inserted all the foreign symbols and accent marks—thank you, Ed. Special thanks to Robert Criso. We met around the manuscript. We now meet for friendship.

Luther Wilson, Director, University of New Mexico Press— receptive to the manuscript, uplifting the witness. Thank you.

Thank you my friend Manna for being my friend Manna.

At a time when dying was a release when "the conditions in the Fascist Concentration Camps were terrible, every cultural activity was a sign of resistance and a will to live."

—Monika Herzog, *Drawings of Ravensbrück*

The drawings in this book were made by imprisoned women of Ravensbrück. Some, during their imprisonment and others shortly after liberation, because many of their sketches were lost or destroyed by the SS. To draw these camp scenes was forbidden. The women risked their lives in secretly "organizing" paper and pencil to depict these terrible conditions. These images should jolt us into remembrance, warning, and action.

I am deeply grateful to Mahn-und Gedenkstatte Ravensbrück for their kind permission to reproduce the drawings shown in this book. The drawings were taken from *Drawings of Ravensbrück* published by the Museum in 1993 and edited by Monica Herzog. Two of those drawing are from the collection of the Museum Der Landeshauptstadt Schwerin. I thank them also for granting permission.

# Preface

   that they should know
those blessed by God
and well-shod fathers
should know

   of shoeless fathers
ashen boys
sated dogs
and shorn women

   know of
polluted skies
blinding the angels
and hiding
God

The lecture on "Religion and the Terror of History" focusing on the Holocaust is over. My history is not. My history is triggered. After class I stand in a line of students at Princeton University, where I, a recent retiree, sit in on courses. When my turn comes I hand Professor Davíd Carrasco, my brief four written lines—my reactions of long ago to God and the Holocaust—the reactions of a Ravensbrück Concentration Camp survivor.

> God, that particular pain
> is too much for me
> You have it and
> be branded

Carrasco is immediately interested and asks if I would talk to the class about my Holocaust experiences. Amazingly, I nod yes. Amazingly to me. It is now 1998, some fifty-three years after the war, and I have kept silent. Silent to the world, silent to friends, and especially silent to family. Inside me—the images, noises, brutalities of that world are present. Always. Reprieves are always subject to countless triggers—bread, snow, a child, hair, gray hair, a dog. The absence of things, the presence of things. Triggers. There are no non-triggers.

> survivorship territory
> multiple residences
> lived in simultaneously
> this place — that other place.
> I say it is now far enough
> late enough
> to live here now,
>     so let the showers
>     be just that, and the railway tracks,
>         potatoes too — see, they are plentiful
> but how do you disconnect from KZ Ravensbrück?

It takes me fifty years to say Kaddish for my parents. Ele dies in concentration camp Sachsenhausen, Germany. Ilona in transit camp Sered, Czechoslovakia. For one year at 6:00 every morning

I say Kaddish. Traditionally, a son should say this memorial prayer, but their son, Karpu, is gassed in Auschwitz at age nine. My Kaddish is a ritual recognition, an external acceptance of my parents' Apu and Anyu's death. For full acceptance you need witnessing, shovelling soil into the open grave pit

> I wish for a cemetery with gravestones
> with the name of... with the name of...
> with the name of...
> Lord, it would help if You would light some candles
> say Kaddish

They die in their early forties—I at fourteen am certainly not equipped for their death. Their murder. Not then and not today.

> I am old in this late year
> but my soul — my soul
> is peopled with parents
> who are younger than my children.
> My brother will forever be nine

1995. I return to Ravensbrück. Survivors of Ravensbrück and nearby Sachsenhausen Concentration Camps are invited by Germany to commemorate the 50th anniversary of the liberation. My husband, Reuven, comes with me. In the Ravensbrück museum guest book I write, "I know of my struggle about 'telling' my children. What do you Ravensbrück SS tell your children?"

> Do you say
> obedience is the law
> the law is loyalty
> us — Über Alles?
> Do you have nightmares
> with the boots polished of stains

under your bed?
Do you tell your children
of the children
who stained your boots?
Do you have nightmares?

We return to the U.S. on the day our Synagogue is holding a Yom Hashoah, a Holocaust commemoration service. When I call the Rabbi to ask if I could participate in the service, he agrees. Is surprised. "This is the first time Survivors volunteer to speak." In years past I would not even join in the processional candle-lighting ceremony.

A survivor of Auschwitz speaks first. He speaks in Yiddish. Though most congregants do not understand the words, they understand the language. It is in their soul. It is the language through which he connects himself and us to his other world, in which he lives today. Always.

Excerpts of my remarks in accented English—reactions to the return:

"...on the Lufthansa plane going there, while still on the ground at Kennedy Airport, I ask the stewardess for water—to impress upon myself that this is a different journey from my last one to Ravensbrück—in the wagon train from Czechoslovakia over fifty years ago.

"...in the dinning room of the German country inn near Sachsenhausen and Ravensbrück, a Jewish ex-prisoner says to the German owner, "*Wir können Heute kein Brot essen, wir sind Juden, es ist Pesach.*" We cannot eat bread today, we are Jews, it is Passover. Shortly, *matzot* and kosher wine are brought to us. A normal interaction, but to me—mind blowing. An Exodus experience.

"...I send a postcard to myself from Ravensbrück—to a home address that will be unchanged when I return.

"...in Sachsenhausen I say Kaddish for my father Ele, and his brother, Moshe, both murdered there. I want them to know that

I said Kaddish at the memorial grave pit under the Israeli flag. Lord, you should see to this.

"...I also place a flower on the lake in Ravensbrück where the ashes of the crematoria are dumped. A flower for those who have no one to place a flower for them."

Ora, our youngest child says, "You tell us nothing about your experiences so everything I hear or read about the Holocaust I imagine happened to you." So it is—I have the experiences, she has the imaginings.

> Ora, it is my ardent wish to be a "mother, oh yes a mother,
>
>     you can stand
>
>     up to"

and yet, you see me in that world of branding and shaming and vulnerabilities. And my own silence amplifies these horrors for you. Such a burden is unfair.

Consequently, a year later, in 1996, I agree to recount my story to the Shoah Oral History Foundation. I send a copy of the video-tape to each of our three children.

The tape is filmed in the privacy of our living room. My earlier Yom Hashoah remarks are limited to reactions of the Ravensbrück return. It is in Carrasco's class at Princeton two years later that I talk for the first time to a live audience about my ACTUAL Holocaust experience.

Carrasco propels me from silence to voice. He brings his brilliant teaching—his classes fill auditoriums—and his mighty size (six-foot-one, two hundred) to the "Terror of History." He pays attention. He does not protect himself, nor his students, nor me. He lets the terror of history terrify.

Carrasco, thank you for facilitating my movement from silence to sound, from telling to writing.

My story is relatively benign compared to others, but not so are the images I carry of those others. I know thirst, separation, degradation, cold, powerlessness—know as only a survivor of a Lager knows. Knows the depths of hunger and crushing cold. But my story is only partial, I do not know the enormity of it. Only Anyu and Apu, Karpu, Yidu, Moshe, Irenke, the named and the unnamed know the final of the Final Solution.

And the perpetrators? And bystanders?

Accountability is Divinity.

This story should not have happened—it did. We believed such stories cannot happen again—they are. Genocide, ethnic cleansing. Witnesses of Auschwitz, tellers of Ravensbrück, the mutilated of Rwanda, the murdered of Bosnia. Terrors of history. Terrors ongoing.

World, I have a question.
World of ethnic cleansing —
Who is clean?

## Say the Name

Say the name
Announce pronounce
Recite the name
Six Million times the name, the name

You master race
Who smashed and gassed
   — erased the name
Script, engrave
Imprint the name
And say and say and say the name,
When every name is said and heard
Repeat the name again again

May you outlive eternity
And say the name eternally
God, please attend
God, please assure
That every name
Is accounted for

# *Chapter One*

## Home in Kurima

A brook runs through the center of the main street. On each side is an alley of acacia trees—providing elegance and shade. On Shabbat afternoons we stride back and forth, back and forth, along this pathway. Wearing our best and noting everyone else's best. Everyone knows everyone—guests too. Shabbat preparations start on Wednesday with a seriousness of purpose and no short cuts. So now, after prayers, meals and nap time, we *shpatzir*, we stroll. Predictably and pleasantly.

The river. The river on the south side of the meadow. The meadow—a carpet of wild flowers. The river runs the mill. We splash and run in the river. My brother, sister, cousins, all the village population.

Somewhere in Czechoslovakia, you can still find this place. I did—again. After Auschwitz and Ravensbrück. After London, Jerusalem, America. After marriage, children, and grandchildren. I went back,

View of Kurima, my hometown. Photo by author.

the house not there
the plum trees in the garden
recognize me.

**Kurima.** Kurima is not marked on the world map, not even on the national map. It is marked only on the local map. Kurima is a very local place. A place unto itself with connections to the outside as needed, for dental visits, search for a teacher, telephone installer, wife for the rabbi. Some leave to marry, others come to marry. My mother, Ilona, and her cousin, Irenke, come from the west to marry two brothers; Moshe, the older, and Ele, my father. In summer adult children and grandchildren come to visit parents and relatives. Our house always has summer guests. Aunt Frieda comes yearly from Kosice with her two children, Trudi and Nisu. She brings ribbons and does our hair in the "latest style."

Kurima is central to us and I feel precociously central in it.

> the wheat in my father's field
> bowed to my father's child
> when I was eight

Ours is an extended family. Paternal grandparents, their two sons and their families. Three children in Moshe's family and four in ours. The maid sleeps in the kitchen; all the other rooms have two or more occupants. Full house, always.

We own a general store, fields, forests, partnership in a brick factory.

We have aspirations and expect them to be fulfilled.

## Grandfather

> A man who can peel
> an apple with glee
> undisturbed, unperturbed
> graciously disrobing
> peel from core
> knows
> how life
> flows

Israel Stern sits by the window of the front room. The pipe is long-handled so that his right hand is stretched out—to reach the bowl of the pipe. No one else in the family smokes. He is the only man in the family with a beard—speckled gray, seldom trimmed. His suits are always black, his shirts always white.

The view from the window provides a large enough circumference of what he needs of this world now—a predictably pleasing outside seen from a caring, comfortable inside. He does not ask questions and comes silently to table for meals. Ambition and curiosity have been fully satisfied. He built this house, founded the store, jumpstarted the synagogue. All now in the good hands of his sons.

But there is one thing he continues to do, and do well. He puts down the pipe to peel the apple. One thin continuous swirling peel uncovers the whole apple, and we who watch finally release our held-in breath. He then cuts the apple into even slices for those present. There are bushels full of cool apples in the basement, but only this one is blessed with grandfather's smirky, loving, show-off labor. Did he build his estate like this—with total focus, skill, and others in mind?

Israel Stern dies when he is ready to leave the window seat, when this sphere no longer engages him. There is quiet acceptance of his loss.

We leave his pipe on the windowsill.

## Serious Men

In my small town
where the river runs deep
the red-haired miller
his two sons and son-in-law
serious men
with serious tasks
place sacks of barley
corn and rye
before serious men
whose serious task
is done

This good season
saw grain to flour

Brook running through center of Kurima. Photo by author.

women folk will
make the bread
— all will smell the bread
and smile,
a serious Amen smile

Our good, bread-filled world.

**Apu.** My father, Apu, loves the land. He does not work it; the store demands his labor. But the land elicits his passion, curiosity, his lightness, his intensity. Apu is a slight, slim man, not a big eater. But food production, grain growing, absorbs him. The fields anchor him. His forests are for green pleasure. The fields for seriousness and serious satisfaction. The land is spread over several villages as is the custom with land ownership. Apu tracks to the various fields at times of seeding, plowing, harvesting, and in between.

Anyu says, "It is three o'clock, don't wake the girls."

Apu says, "They want to come along. I know they want to come along."

Anyu, "Let them sleep. They will forgive you."

Apu, "I will not forgive myself. They will miss an important outing."

He wakes Elza and me. His pockets are filled with hazel nuts, chocolates, almonds, and raisins. Traditional treats for these events. For cousin Elza and me, these are annual pilgrimages of sweets and hayrides. We also accompany the grain to the mill and if there is time, pick wild strawberries in the forest. Back home in time for breakfast, with Elza and I invigorated by the adventure, Apu does not say, "I told you so." And Anyu pretends not to hear.

The land our family owns is laced with Apu's presence. I do not know how long the land has been in the family, but it has always been in him.

He plans to buy land in Israel.

## Wild Strawberries

Going home to
mother

carefully guarding
the wild strawberries

I picked that dawn
dew covered still

she is clad in blue
matching the blue pitcher

pouring buttermilk
for the potato pickers

**Are we wealthy?** We do expect our aspirations to be fulfilled. The family has a reputation for being wealthy. Our standard of living is not luxurious, but I have a sense that we have enough and the future is assured. Saving for the future is very serious, hardly discussed, but fully assumed. I see our wealth evidenced in three areas. Cousin Elza and I have to distribute envelopes with money to several families before each major festival and special occasion, such as illnesses or weddings. This task has to be done very unobtrusively. A secret, not just from others, even the family receiving the money is not to know from whom the gift is coming. We either push the envelope under the outside door, or, if we should visit, the envelope is left somewhere—casually—to be found after we leave. I do not know if the recipient is fooled, but our family tradition of anonymous giving is maintained.

The second proof of our wealth—people from outlying areas, who come to pray in our synagogue on Shabbat or festivals, always eat with us. Third, when a poor relative gets engaged or married, we provide the dowry and pay for the affair. We also provide the drapes that separate the women's from the men's section of the synagogue. A luxurious fabric of deep gold velvet with a green trim.

And the surest sign of prosperity—no hand-me-downs.

Aunt Irenke chooses the fabrics for our dresses and takes us girls to the dressmaker. We are allowed to choose the style, but have to negotiate this among ourselves because both fabric and style have to be the same for all of us. Our brothers too wear matching clothing. Our mothers have their dresses made in town. I am always convinced that they are the two best-dressed women in the village, and the prettiest.

Details are taken seriously. Attention is paid to details. We specialize in details. Anyu's sister Yolanka visits every summer. She is dainty, elegant, and single. Unlike our other guests, she does not help out, nor is she expected to. Anyu caters to her with special care. A recliner chair is placed for her under the plum tree. She is served bananas, a rare delicacy. We children respect her need " for rest and quiet." She is served Shabbat pastries the whole week. She receives special treatment and she brings specialness into our lives. My sister Mirjam gets a lavender doll's carriage. I am given a deep blue, suede-covered autograph book.

Yolanka writes into it: "Enjoy the joy of the moment—"

Anyu's other sister, Shari, lives in the nearby town of Bardejov. We visit when we go to the dentist. She never visits, but her children do. Shari looks sad and tired. Her husband never speaks to us. To Shari, Anyu sends money.

Life for the adults in the family is busy. Not harsh, not deprived, but active and responsible. Yolanka's bananas; the anonymous envelopes; grandmother's baking every family member's favorite delicacy. We specialize in details.

Later Yolanka writes, "Earlier I wrote . . . enjoy the joy of the moment . . . now I am asking, do you?"

She too, the details.

And then terror. German soldiers are rampaging through the house in the middle of the night.

A gun with a bayonet is pointed at my sleeping head
a nightmare this — but it is real
happening when
I am not quiet ten.
Why is he here — this soldier — with the grin and gun
who yells at us in loud German?
"Relax you pigs — you Jewish kids
you are safe for now
the person we want — is the man with the beard
to the man with the beard
we have come to deliver a wunderbar treat!"

In the hall against the wall
a gun is aimed at every head
of uncles, aunts, my mom and dad.
"Where is he hiding that man with the beard
it will not go well if you do not tell!"
They finally leave — they finally go
now all of us know — the taste and the feel
of TERROR and FEAR.

I hear my mother say, "Shoot us or leave us alone." How does she dare? Eventually the soldiers leave, not because of her words—it is not yet time to shoot Jews in Czechoslovakia. In Poland it is. That is where these troops are headed, to complete the occupation of Poland. 1939.

**Omama.** Omama, grandmother, wants to live. I am in the next room and hear her protesting, moaning, calling. Calling, "Moshe, Ele, Irene, Ilon, Frieda." She calls and calls. She also calls me, "Hanele." She does not want to leave. She wants everyone to be near her, to hold on to. Omama is too connected to this world to leave. The doctor is with her, as are all the adults. I am scared to go in there.

She is a protester, a doer; resignation is not for her.

There are things I know because of her. I can distinguish the green carrot leaves from parsley leaves. Know when tomatoes should be picked—right before they ripen. Know weeds from plants. How to stake sweet peas. Know the movements of potato pickers. I know Modeh Ani, the morning prayer, and Shema, the evening prayer.

Though we are an Orthodox Jewish family, Omama puts a Christmas tree in the kitchen for the maid, who sleeps there.

Omama is very practical. My mother is very respectful of her in all ways—except when it comes to the flowerbeds. Mother wants more garden space and Omama is loathe to shrink her vegetable patch. Increasingly the flowerbed widens. Anyu makes me put fresh flowers on Omama's night table—ANONYMOUSLY.

Omama is very practical, but she beautifies practicality. She puts freshly homemade butter into a brown earthenware bowl and with a wooden spoon makes a design of half moon shapes. Only the deep blue pitcher will do for the buttermilk. She is frugal, but when a poor man eats at our house, she prepares a care package upon his leaving. True, food does not enter into her sphere of frugality. Every week she bakes everyone's favorite pastry, in addition to the bread and challah.

She does not tolerate idleness. We grandchildren try to avoid induction into weeding. We do not linger after summer lunches. But she knows our moves and is ready for us, especially cousins Elza, Mella, and me. Vicariously, she also enjoys our unweeding activities and likes to hear about them in detail, village gossip included, especially village gossip.

Omama's roots are in the big city. One brother is a distinguished rabbi in Hamburg, Germany. The other is a professional in Presov. Large places compared to Kurima. But her sinews are Kurima honed. She out-natives the natives. She never leaves the place, but those she cares about reciprocate. They visit—her children, grandchildren, relatives, all stay with us, live with us, leave and come back to us.

Like everyone in the family, Omama speaks four or five languages, a consequence of the ever-changing history of the region. Within the family there is a ritualized division of languages. The shift from one to another to another is effortless, spontaneous. We children speak:

Yiddish with grandparents. (In the family only Anyu and Irenke do not speak Yiddish.)

German with fathers.

Hungarian with mothers.

Slovak in school, with friends, villagers, etc.

We also study Hebrew in Hebrew School and Zionist clubs.

During these times of persecution and deportation, the adults, in their protectiveness, withhold bad news from Omama. "Hanele, what is going on? You tell me." She pulls me toward her, eager for answers. Hannah is my Hebrew name. She calls us all by our Hebrew names: Elka, Feige, Miru, Karpu, and Yidu.

"In Russia the German army has *planmässig zurückgezogen*," I quote for her the headlines from the paper. The German army has retreated according to plan.

"But what else? What about here in Slovakia? In Kurima?" she demands.

"*Jetzt ist ruhig. Jetzt shiktmen nisht*," I say with a somewhat clear conscience. Most people have already been deported and there is a tense untrusting quiet.

"Why don't they tell me all? *Tzu zein, mis men vissen.*" To exist one must know. It is so sad to hear her beg for involvement. With no power or function, she is an old woman. She lived a life of being in charge. She made things happen. She was central. She dealt with busy times. Hard times. Shabbat times. Doing, deciding, overseeing—her lifelong tools. I spend more time with her now, but try to discuss neutral matters.

Omama dies. The family sits *shiva*. Because most Jews have already been deported, there is now barely a *minyan*—barely ten men available—for the required Kaddish service. Her children mourn not mourning. They mourn the relief they feel that she dies at home. They almost celebrate that she has a burial, a gravestone, Kaddish. We do not know the fate of the old people who left. But none were brought back for burial in their own cemetery—next to those they knew or their parents knew or someone knew.

Katerina Sternova, you should not have to be deprived of the lamentations due you. We should take a stand and proclaim this is your place; this is where you lived and died. Here we celebrate your life—your useful, tenacious life. Here we mourn your death—freely, becomingly. This should be said, this should be heard.

Omama, your grandchildren know the smell and taste of homemade bread, the Shema, and the gift to the maid of a Christmas tree in the kitchen.

## Two cemeteries

In my small town
with the lazy brook
two cemeteries
back to back
one with script
from right to left
the other with signs
of Mary and child

Two cemeteries
back to back
the folks therein
they know — they know
love of neighbor
peace on earth
exist in the abode
under — groumd

**The Town Crier.** The Town Crier brings the news. Marching, he drums an even steady beat, then speeds up the rhythm when stopping at the designated place under a tree. By now people will have gathered and he reads solemnly from the paper in his possession. Hear ye, hear ye—the voice is the same no matter what the content. He does not answer questions nor repeats the message. His is the most structured ritual in the village. His behavior remains the same, but in these times the content changes. In the past the news was universal, it applied to the whole village population. A bridge to be built. A meeting about bringing in electricity. Information regarding the annual May Day parade.

Now the announcements are directed mainly at Jews. The whole population still comes to listen. Some come with glee, some with embarrassment, some with curiosity, and some with indifference. Jews come with trepidation. News regarding Jews is in the foreground. Normal village business no longer applies to us—connections are increasingly loosened and then severed.

Mockingly, marching behind the Town Crier, irreverently beating on non-existent drums, assuming exaggerated listening positions, we children used to make theatrics out of the situation. Not now. Now we stand silently, closely watching our parents' anxious reactions and picking up their fear and worry.

Jews must give up their business, transfer land ownership, restrict travel, wear a yellow star, hand in valuables. The Town Crier repeats these orders in several places, as though this news would not travel fast enough on its own. It gets there before he does.

The drums predict peril. The Town Crier is neutral. The message hateful.

We take the silver Shabbat candlesticks to the police station. Hand over grandfather's Kiddush cup, a gift from his father. Jewelry. Fur shawls, fur collars. Silverware, engravings. What will they do with these? What is the value of two silver candlesticks minus two generations of Shabbat blessings? Will the silver be sold by weight?

God, make an accounting.

Grandma is sad, she has lost the right
to her Shabbat light,
then grandma says, "God, do not fret
I will make a light
that is brighter yet"

she lights the candles on a stone
and adds to this her special glow,

She will not deprive God of His blessing.

Some valuables are held back and, late at night, are secretly buried in the garden behind the house. Engagement rings, bracelets, pocket watches—family valuables and family history. Fabrics and some other items from the store are secretly carried over to Christian neighbors for hiding. In return they are given some of the merchandise. A few want more and some refuse any payment. The family income now depends on secret sales and barter. But we have enough for now.

**We go where we are not wanted.** Cousin Elza and I visit Bardejovske Kupele—a spa resort nearby. Elza is older by one year. She is twelve. She has always been the leader of siblings, cousins, and friends. She is daring and adventurous, and I do not want to miss out. Bardejovske Kupele is forbidden to Jews.

"What about the star?" I ask.

"They do not want stars there. So we go without!" Elza says flippantly.

We risk discovery and punishment if apprehended without the star and we risk abuse and punishment if caught with it. A dress without the star it is. Our parents are naturally not informed of our plans. We walk to the next village where we are not known and hitch a ride from there.

The many hotels in Bardejovske Kupele are now occupied by Hitler Jugend, youth from Germany. They wear short black pants, brown shirts, black ties, and knee high socks. They wear polished shoes and polished buckles. The high polish matches their shiny confidence. They ooze entitlement. They march to energizing marching songs along the street, the street where we formerly strolled with ice cream and large salty pretzels. I envy their starless strutting chests, loud voices, and unapologetic visibility. In letters home, do they "Heil Hitler" and brag about racial superiority to stupid Slavs and damned, *verfluchte* Jews? They feast in our country and glorify the Fatherland.

Soon, with ice cream in hand, Elza and I mingle and pretend legitimacy, though not with the same confidence as these presumptuous Hitler Youth. Not wearing the star expands my chest. I strut in its absence. I am light, free, rambunctious. I relish visibility. We enter hotel lobbies and churches. We sit on "No Jews Permitted" benches. We adopt the fearless identities of German youth and Slovak Christians. The weightlessness of not being Jewish.

When we arrive home after dark... "If you ever, ever do a thing like that again!"... relieved reprimand from parents. They know of our daring adventure from a villager who had seen us there.

But Elza and I continue to go places where we are not wanted— but we continue to want.

Ironically, a very daring and desperate young relative also goes where he is not wanted. Cousin Yossi joins a branch of the Hitler Jugend. He speaks German well and assumes a German Aryan identity. On the day he is seen in the shower he barely, just barely makes his escape. I witness the scene of his homecoming. His mother slaps him. "How could you put me through this!" Then hugs and kisses him. Another relative, cousin Dudi, works for the Gestapo in Bratislava, the capital, while secretly serving in the Resistance movement. He is caught, tortured, and executed. His mother is not here to reprimand. She is already deported, as is his father. Dudi's two siblings in Israeli Kibbutzim name children after him.

**The officer.** The German Wehrmacht officer enters the classroom of our Jewish school. He is polite, removes his hat and addresses our teacher with the formal "Sie." We all gather around the teacher's desk to hear them talk

Officer: "What do you think of our plan for the Jews? Our Führer will give you a homeland in Madagascar."

Teacher: "That will not be necessary. We already have a homeland in Palestine."

Officer: *"Na, das weiss ich nicht."* I don't know about that.

Teacher: *"Das weiss ich, ja."* I do know about that.

Shaking his head, the officer leaves. Our teacher is our hero, though we are not yet fully aware of the uniqueness of this interaction. A Jewish teacher who dares disagree with a German officer, and a German officer who allows it. There is not likely to be a repeat performance during the reign of the Third Reich.

We can no longer attend public school. Hitler says Jewish children contaminate the air and "Aryan children must be protected from such pollution." Though the public school teachers are not rejoicing at this latest proclamation, neither do they protest. A Jewish elder protests to the Chief of Police. "I don't like this either, but it is the law. What can I do?" says the Chief.

**It is the law**

It is the law
is the law
out of my hands
it is the law

how, in all those
hymnal holding
hands
    impotence?

We learn in a one-room schoolhouse. Eight grades in one room. Our new teacher manages and teaches. Her salary is small, she is paid by the Jewish community which is by now largely unemployed. The State no longer funds Jewish schools. I like this school.

There is never any physical punishment. We are not all good students, but we all behave well. Good behavior is not optional—mandated by parents. Older students help the younger ones. And since the teacher has no colleagues, we stand around her desk at break times and inquire about her skiing, at which she excels, and pry about her romantic involvements with Jacob. She enjoys not commenting on our creatively spun romantic tales.

I miss only the view from my public school. It faces the meadow leading to the river. The Jewish school overlooks a brick building and depleted garden patches.

> my meadow grows poppies and daisies
> and flowers
> so blue —
> there isn't a color
> my meadow won't do

The school is held in the Beit Hamidrash—the house of study—connected to the synagogue. Next to it lives our young rabbi with his wife and his infant son. The rabbi is new to this position, but his legacy dates to his birth, as the eldest son of the previous rabbi. Upon the recent death of his father he assumes his role, like royalty. He brings back a beautiful wife from Žilina, further enhancing his position and our community.

The Rebbetzin sits on the bench in front of her house wearing a long satin, flowered, caftan-like dress, rocking the baby carriage and talking about "the city." I do not envy her the city but understand her hidden yearning for it. Should I ever marry out of Kurima such will also be my longing. I do feel a little resentful, though, that she does not transfer her feelings onto our village. She refers to her husband reverently, "the Rabbi," and there is love in her sound.

She loves Žilina, and she loves our rabbi. Good enough.

℮〜

**Enemy language.** Anyu and I visit friends in a nearby village, a Christian family with teen-aged sons. When we get there, Yuro, the youngest wants to practice his German. Would we talk to him? Yuro is destined for a university education—a rare goal among children of this farm population. On prior visits the father would show us Yuro's high math and science grades. Now the school is teaching German and Yuro wants to do well. Though we speak German at home, in this house German is the language of the enemy. Enemy language from the mouths of friends. We do not help Yuro with his practice of German.

On the way home Anyu wonders, "Will they make us give up German? What will I read?" On her night-table are always the same two books by Schiller and Goethe. She reads other books but always goes back to these, like Omama to her Bible. Luckily Anyu knows other languages, for soon Jews are not allowed German books.

Instead we are forced to buy a series of vicious anti-semitic books depicting alleged Jewish perversions and conspiracies. The cartoons are nightmarish. Apu suggests we do what the Germans do and burn the abominable books. We do not burn them. Neither do we read them. But pay for them we must . . . as was required after Kristallnacht in Germany, when Jews had to pay for the organized destruction of their own property.

**The Star.** The wearing of a yellow star is an absurd order in Kurima. Every one here knows who is a Jew, a Christian, knows everyone's home address, number of children, number of horses in the barn, down to even the paint color of everyone's house. But now what is known has different meaning. Before, we take our Jewishness for granted—like the color of our eyes, a given reality. The star introduces a demarcation, a badge of shame. A Jew with a star is a different Jew. No one is indifferent to a yellow Jewish star, not a

Christian observer, not a Jewish wearer. Its intent is branding and shaming. It provokes ridicule and abuse from the outside—humiliation and shame and rage from within. For my Christian friends my star becomes the foreground—our commonality replaced with exaggerated differences. The star proclaims Jews are different and inferior. A distance develops.

Accommodations of several generations wiped out within days by a small piece of yellow cloth. Now that we are branded, they find it easier to enforce other brutal rules.

# Chapter Two

# Deportations

The town crier announces deportations will take place. The language used—"resettlement to the East." More information is not provided, except for the luggage allowed—one suitcase per person. The deportations are by categories: young people, men, families with no specified exemptions, and on.

**Szuri.** Szuri lives with her grandmother. Just the two of them. Her parents died several years ago. Szuri is twelve. Her grandmother— I do not know—but she seems very old and frail. Szuri and grandmother are among the first families to be deported. I am there to—to—to be there. We do not say goodbye because we do not yet comprehend what deportation is. Szuri stands in the small front room fingering the needlepoint picture on the wall. Her mother made it. The frame is oval and not very large, but Szuri has no room in her suitcase. "It will be here after the war," she says, stroking it gently. She leaves to help her grandmother down the steps and into the waiting truck.

Very shortly after, village people loot the house. A villager looks at the needlepoint picture, and then throws it onto the heap on the floor with the other no longer valued items. The glass shatters and the frame breaks. He takes with him the coffeepot and umbrella.

I stand hidden behind the drapes and cry—for Szuri, because she is not here to do her own crying.

**Evka's request.** Only a handful of Jewish families are left in the village. My friend Evka's family is scheduled for the next transport. Evka comes by with a request.

"As soon as we get there, I will send our new address to you so you can send us Papa's letters," she says.

"I will," I reply. "But why don't you send the address to him directly?"

She looks hurt. "Papa is used to writing to this address. Promise you will check for his letter every day at the post office. I told them to give it to you." I promise.

Evka badly wants Papa's letters, and she is equally concerned that they not be sent back to him, lest he stop writing.

Papa's letters come only about two to three times a year. Her father left for America seven years ago. The plan was that he would send for the family as soon as he saved up the fares. Evka was five and her brother Isaac was three when he left. In every letter he states the tickets will arrive "soon." Every letter brings hope and disappointment. Evka knows him by the one tinted photograph he sent. It is in a silver plated frame on a small lace covered table. Out of hurt and frustration her mother turns the photograph face down when Evka leaves for school—then, on her return from school, Evka rightens it. This regular ritual is never discussed. They are sweetly protective of each other while from far away America Papa keeps the hurt and hopes alive. Maternal grandparents keep the family fed.

I pick up one letter from the post office, but receive no forwarding address. Evka must not have an address.

At what point are the letters no longer delivered? No longer written? What does he make of this—that papa in America whose photograph in Kurima moves from upright to downright to upright?

**Brothers.** Two brothers go into hiding. They are our youth leaders. They hide in the attic above the Beit Hamidrash—House of Learning. Their parents and siblings are already deported. Baruch is twenty, Hershi eighteen. Baruch, the artist and ardent Zionist draws and distributes posters saying, "Away with the White Paper." He is enraged at the British betrayal of the Balfour Declaration and their drastic limitation of Jewish immigration to Palestine. Baruch teaches us about Palestine and supplements our religious teachings with Zionist aspirations. Hershi idolizes and looks up to his brother. We all do. Baruch, handsome with curly hair and serious agendas is the object of infatuation of every girl and role model for every boy.

While the brothers are in hiding, our family sends food to them. Elza and I are the deliverers. If we are stopped, we are to say, "We are afraid of deportations and are running away from home. The food is for our dinner." This is early in the deportation season and there is as yet no concern that we two young girls would not be returned to our parents if caught. The police are still on good terms with our family.

For several months we two manage our deliveries successfully, but one day we find the secret attic door open and the attic empty. Our friends are sent "to the East."

**Best friends and bicycles.** Ruthie and I love being together, we confirm and reaffirm a thousand times each other's best friend status—now and forever. We have strong opinions about who in the village should marry whom and equally whom they should not marry, how long the engagements should last. We check to see whose breasts are developing faster (hers). We pronounce absolute judgment about boys' looks. Regarding who is the teacher's pet, I say little—guiltily and pleasingly suspecting that I am. Ruthie invariably brings up the subject. She has new ice skates and longer braids—that evens us out in my estimation.

But bicycles strain our friendship. Uncle Moshe brings bicycles for sale into our store. Mr. Treitel, Ruthie's father, owns a bicycle store. I am totally sympathetic with Mr. Treitel; he only sells bicycles, whereas our store has such a variety of merchandise. I challenge Uncle Moshe on this and he informs me that after the current shipment is sold out, no more will be ordered. This decision is based on business matters rather than my discomfort, but I am thrilled. When I run with the good news to Mr. Treitel, he is too angry to be pleased.

Ruthie and I never resume our exuberant friendship. Resentment towards Uncle Moshe is transferred unto me. The Treitels feel betrayed by my family and I by Ruthie. She and I are now old enough to discuss more weighty matters, but we do so with less fun and more inhibition.

Soon the bicycle store is taken over by a Nazi sympathizer who does such good business that more such stores are opened and competition is strong. Jews have to give up their bicycles. I do not care—bicycles marred our friendship. Ruthie and her family are deported. More unfinished business with no opportunities for correction. My world is shrinking. Ruthie, Szuri, Evka, where is your world? Where?

**What to take?** Prior to deportations we are told to pack fifteen kilograms of belongings per person. Not more. It would be much easier to go into a store with a list of essential items than to select from a lived-in home.

Photographs?

No, they will get crumpled.

The candlesticks?

Too heavy, these of brass. The silver ones have been confiscated already.

Mother's monogrammed sheets?

Moshe's pure wool Tallit?

An iron? A sewing kit?

Irenke's newly acquired book, *Gone with the Wind*?

Karpu's harmonica?

How many socks? Gloves?

Prayer books? Report cards? Passports? Pen-knife?

Elza's autograph book? Mine?

Winter coats? Boots? What climate there? Where?

We have furniture, a carved mirror, wine decanter, a butter churner. In this mirror we test new hair-styles. Our family history is in these things. Our family history is woven through them. We belong to them and to the chairs, and stairs, the cat and plum trees. We know the connections. What was acquired, when, by whom. Who made what. How the dents occurred. Our prints are on everything. These belongings were not acquired in one sudden move. They grew as the family grew. These belongings proclaim choices, hesitations, sweetness ...generosity, frugality, savings and extravaganzas. Pride and productivity and rituals and traditions. These belongings are cherished because of their connections. Because they are peopled.

You, who will fatten yourself on our riches, may you be impoverished.

Food—we should take food.

Plum jam—glass jars impractical. Ditto honey.

Eggs, milk, butter—spoil easily.

In the end—dry rice, dry beans, dry crackers, dried coffee beans. We are moving into dryness.

Shirts, flashlight, toothpaste, soap, notepaper, mug, passports are added, and underwear.

The bundles are carried up into the attic. Each bundle has a person's name.

I complain. "I don't like rice or beans or that other stuff. I do not drink that kind of coffee!"

Anyu. "That is only for emergencies. Come, eat your supper."

I do not. That menu up there—fear constricts my throat.

We never make use of those provisions. To avoid deportation we escape, we hide, we impersonate. When eventually caught, the bundles in the attic are inaccessible.

**Resistance.** We, in our family, resist deportation. Talk of avoiding it is constant. There is a determination that we survive—all of us. Some of us. One of us. Our passports to Palestine (Asia Minor) are of no use. The British will not let us in. It is hard for me to conceptualize that we as a family may cease to exist. When my older sister, Olga, dies of pneumonia two years earlier, the family is devastated. When during deportations grandmother dies, there is almost a celebration ...

A sick person dies. An old person dies. But how does a young healthy family no longer exist?

**Escape into Hungary.** Our family is determined to resist. Determined to continue being in charge in spite of their taking all our power away. Five generations of our family has lived within these familiar surroundings, lived within its laws. Now we will have to survive in spite of its changed laws and hostile surroundings. Now our family will separate to remain whole.

For safety, we six children—three siblings from each family—are to be sent across the border into Kassau, now Hungary.

Until 1939 Kassau is known as "Kosice." Our independent Democratic Republic of Czechoslovakia, founded in 1918 after the disintegration of the Austro-Hungarian Empire, is so vital, so optimistic, and so short-lived. Hitler invades in 1939. Czechoslovakia is divided. Czechia is occupied by the German army and Slovakia declares itself an ally of Hitler. Hungary makes a treaty with Germany and is unoccupied. Among the parts of Czechoslovakia ceded to Hungary, is Kosice, renamed Kassau. Aunt Frieda and Uncle Laci are cut off from our Kurima family. Their textile business is taken from them and Uncle Laci's parents are deported to Poland. They are defined as aliens, since they are Polish-born. These aliens lived in Kosice for over fifty years. The world is being re-defined, the people re-labelled. And terror rules. And luck. And luck.

"Will you and Apu come and visit?" I ask Anyu.

"No, that would be too risky. You must say that your parents are dead."

"I do not want to say that! I never will! Never!"

She stops packing the few belongings we are to take with us and seats me on the bed next to her.

"Juditkam, we must do everything possible not to be deported. That is why we are sending you children away. If the Hungarians know that you have parents here, they will send you back—or worse—they will deport you."

"Why can't we be deported—together—like other families?" I ask.

She sounds very serious and determined. "You must promise me to do all you can not to be deported. We do not know where they are sending us, but we hear rumors. It is not safe. And you must also help the other children in our family."

"Can I write to you?"

"No." She has tears in her eyes. "No one here must know where you are."

I try again. "How will Mirjam manage? Mirjam will need you." Mirjam is six.

Anyu, "You and Elza will take care of her, and of Karpu and Yidu, and Mella will help. You are our big girls. Here we can no longer protect any of you. We are so fortunate that we have somewhere to send you."

"Where will you go?"

"We will hide, and we will be here when you all come back." Crying, she continues packing.

I do not cry. I hate being a big girl under these circumstances. Sibling responsibility does not appeal to me anyway. (In my efforts to avoid Mirjam's tagging along, I climb out the front window, but she soon catches on and waits for me out there.)

Craziness. We are "fortunate" because we can be sent away?

"Fortunate" are parents who can send their children into risky unknown situations? Family togetherness spells danger. Our world now consists of powerless parents, unprotected children, and intact families who are no longer.

God, is rendering parents powerless to protect their children not a crime against Your creation? Do You not protest? I do not admire Abraham for not protesting to sacrifice Isaac, even for You. Do You agree?

The six of us are each given money and a small bag. We wear coats without the star. Mirjam insists on carrying her own bag. We leave by car and later transfer to a horse drawn carriage. The farmhouse near the border is isolated and seems a thousand hours from home—though it takes only a night and a day to get there. The farm couple give up their bed for us, the wide bed which takes up most of the room. It accommodates all six of us quite comfortably. We are given milk, bread, and bacon for breakfast. None of us are tempted by the bacon—grandmother's Kashrut injunctions are too powerful. For lunch we eat the thick potato soup and leave the sausage.

The first dark rainy night Elza, Yidu and Mirjam leave for the border. The farmer has been instructed by our parents to split us children into two groups. Two siblings and a cousin in each group, two girls and a boy, to make it fair, "just in case." The farmer's brother-in-law, a teenage boy goes along to help. Two days later the weather is again favorably unfavorable, and Mella, Karpu, and I leave the farm. This time the farmer's wife goes along. She gives her young brother instructions about feeding the horses, milking the cows, egg collection. She gives no additional "just-in-case" guidance and I feel greatly reassured of the success of our illegal crossing.

It rains during our three-hour walk. The borders are clear. No guards, no dogs. We arrive in town at about 4:00 a.m. and head for Frieda's place—33 Srobar Utca. The gates to her apartment house are closed. The farmer does not ring the super's bell. Or Frieda's. Not to draw attention. Did he not go through this already with Elza's group?

Why does he not plan a better arrival time? We move away from the building and walk toward the Dome, the beautiful Cathedral-like church at the end of the street. It too is locked.

For an hour—an eternal hour—we five are the most conspicuous moving sight in town. The only human sight. No policeman. No workers. No milkman. No trams yet either. Three of us follow the farmer and wife. How harsh and glaring and terrorizing this unwelcome visibility. Three children in muddy city clothing following two adults in country attire. I see the wisdom of our parents' making only partial payment; the rest upon proof of delivery, for our guides must surely be tempted to disappear into a less conspicuous situation. They walk fast as though trying to escape from us. But perhaps they are also concerned about our safety. Church bells ring.

## Morning Mass

At 5 a.m.
roaming this city

of bolted doors
I hear my intensified heart
outpound the church bells
inviting the faithful
to 6 a.m. mass
come all yea faithful
glorify Him — the Son
(the Jewish Son)

at 6 a.m. will bolted
locks unbolt for me?
at 6 a.m. where will I be?
will I be?

Slowly people appear bringing produce to market, going to mass. In another hour at 6:00 a.m. Frieda's gate opens, as do the other gates. Through the long yard and up the stairs to Frieda's apartment, to safe invisibility.

She and Uncle Laci stare at us unbelieving. They obviously do not expect us—our parents had no way of informing them. Our welcome is assumed—families come through for each other. But what about Elza's group? Where are they? The farmer then hesitantly reports that he does not know. A border guard spotted them, he and his brother-in-law escaped and the children were captured. Frieda is frantic. The deliverers leave. We are given hot chocolate and buttered rolls and Frieda is calling people who are calling police stations and prisons. Happy news. Elza and Mirjam are in a girl's orphanage and Yidu in a home for boys. They are safe, but must stay where they are. Both these institutions are within walking distance of Frieda's home.

The only way Frieda can keep us is to petition the Hungarian authorities for our release. Therefore, we must first be imprisoned. Therefore we must go to Budapest to arrange for this imprisonment in an internment camp. Budapest is eight hours away by train. The next day Frieda, risking her own internment and worse, takes us there.

The people in the camp are friendly. We have a clean bed and enough food. When internees ask about my parents I mumble and change the subject. To official inquiries I report they were deported. Our orphan status is accepted. Survival is increasingly based on lies and pretense. Karpu develops a rash and is placed in the camp hospital. Mella and I visit often. He is the only child in there and enjoys the adult attention. Unlike me, Karpu does not demand attention—but is lit up by it. Karpu is eight.

Frieda comes to visit. She is not allowed in, and we meet at the gate. I cry.

Frieda: "Juditka, why are you crying?"

Juditka: "How can I not cry when I do not have a toothbrush?"

Frieda: "A tooth brush?" she repeats, relieved and smiling.

It is no smiling matter to me. A person without a toothbrush is a person without. A toothbrush starts your day and ends your day—a ritual like a prayer. A physicalness to hold onto. A grounding. Next day Frieda brings a toothbrush and a comb. She takes us back to Kassau where we stay for almost a year. We girls share her daughter Trudy's bed and dresser and Karpu and Yidu become a threesome with her son Nisu. The boys are approximately the same age.

There is no mail to or from home, but we hear indirectly that our parents in Kurima are all right. Since Uncle Laci no longer has a business to occupy him, he and his friends play cards—rummy. But mostly they listen to the radio, intently following the course of the war.

The teacher of my class reminds us daily of the heroism of her husband who is serving in the Hungarian army while the Jews sit safely home. Incorrect! Does no one inform her that though Jews are barred from army service, large numbers of Jewish men are conscripted into hard labor, road building, and carrying supplies to the front? Instead of math we learn patriotic songs. On my own I memorize Hungarian poems to recite to Anyu upon return home.

I am in love with Ari. Teacher, please call on someone in the back so that I will have an excuse to turn around and look at Ari, three desks behind me. She seldom obliges. Our learning is not her primary agenda. We do not elicit her curiosity or engagement. The class serves as audience for her rantings.

Ari's interest in me is deep but not evident.

> I say :  on the beach
>            next to you
>            we make the
>            ocean vulnerable

(though I have never seen an ocean)

> I say:   toss me your tune
>            and I will drum
>            beat it

To Ari I say, "Your shoe is untied." I can tell that from looking down at the floor, blushing. My eloquence remains stuck in my notebook.

Elza, Yidu and Mirjam come for Shabbat, festivals, and whenever they wish. Apart from homesickness, life is very tolerable. We are never made to feel unwelcome. We are accepted and included.

March, 1944. The Germans suddenly occupy Hungary. All Jews are to be deported immediately. Adolf Eichmann comes to Budapest to ensure that the deportations are done efficiently and fast. Our parents manage to have us smuggled back into Czechoslovakia.

**Temporary homecoming.** We return to Kurima—all six of us children. Deportations have resumed; it is not safe. We can stay only a few hours. Mrs.Gruen, the doctor's wife, and Jano, her son, come by. Jano and I feel shy in each other's presence. There is no time to get beyond this, back to earlier camaraderie or to a newer level. Newer it would have to be—I have romance in mind. This longed for return home has none of the fullness I imagined. None of the delighted celebration. No time for our accumulated "telling." No time for my memorized poems. No time for our questions: how was your life during our absence? Where? Which Jewish family is still here? Which of our friends?

I do ask about Frieda and her family. Apu assures me arrangements are made for their escape from Hungary.

Anyu says, "One day we will bring you all home and not send you away again." Mirjam sits on her lap. But on this day, homecoming is only a stop-over for leaving. The threat of the future—the immediate cattle car future—deprives us of any homecoming joy.

No one says let's stay together, come what may. "Come what may," is not in my family's vocabulary. Survival is. Togetherness works against it.

Tessa comes by, my Christian friend, former friend. We sit next to each other in third grade of the public school, before I am expelled. She brings a bushel of potatoes, and my father pays her. Since third grade Tessa's is the only life I know that has followed a predictable course. In the fall she will attend the seventh grade of public school—the right grade in the right school. In summer her father grows potatoes and Tessa helps deliver them.

Within the hour our family leaves our home—in several directions.

# Chapter Three

## Hiding

**E**lza. In a small town 150 kilometers from Kurima a Christian family takes in Elza. Part of their house is soon occupied by German soldiers of the Wehrmacht, the General Army. Elza is a pretty, dark-haired, vivacious teenager. A young German soldier likes her, brings her white leather boots and invites her to come to Germany when the war is over. He writes his mother about Elza and his plans for her.

Elza is renamed Anni. She lives here as a niece "whose mother is sick and cannot look after her." With so much German spoken around her, should she pretend not to understand the language or admit that she does? The family is middle class, the father an engineer. Having a well-educated German-speaking niece would not arouse suspicion. For Elza it would be less stressful not to have this additional pretense.

The German language, which from birth connects Elza to her father, is now silenced. The German language within this world of pretense gives Anni privileged status with the deadly enemy.

Elza's sister, Mella, is taken in by a pastor in another town. She is eleven. She is taught Christian prayers and hymns and attends church regularly with the family. The pastor's three young daughters are told Mella is a niece whose sick mother cannot care for her. The "story" of hidden children does not vary much—will it be accepted?

Always the question. Always the worry.

Fortunate. Elza, Mella, you are fortunate not to live in some cold, dark hiding place. But they nevertheless live anxious lives of pretense. Keeping the story consistent or improvising when questioned by police or suspicious neighbors keeps them on edge. The rescuing families are also at great risk and cannot count on friends or neighbors for support. They too have to be alert for possible betrayals resulting in their own destruction.

You brave, kind families who take in Jews at great risk to yourselves, you are the only good, during this time of evil. Nothing, nothing, else is.

Karpu and Yidu are "somewhere" in hiding with aunt Irenke. It is very hard to find a Christian family who will take in Jewish boys.

**Betrayal.** Mirjam and I are taken in by a Christian family in Presov. We stay in the back room and do not turn lights on at night. The father of the family is alcoholic. He goes through our belongings and takes what money we have. We are not to tell his wife or mother-in-law. After this injunction he is friendly, and basically ignores us. Our food is sufficient. We have no books or radio, no news of the outside. Much of the time we stay in bed, and I make up stories for Mirjam. The days are long. A knock on the door, the sound of a car, everything is suspect. In our restricted world nothing but fear is normal. To the outside observer our room must seem like a crypt. No evening light, no curtain movement, lifeless sameness. But someone is not deceived. We are betrayed.

Boots, a harsh knock, threatening voices. Our door is thrust open. *Raus! Raus! Mach Schnell! Raus!* They drag us into the truck. Three trucks are waiting—a large number of soldiers at the ready. We are taken out so quickly that we do not see what is happening to the family. God, let them not be shot. Please, not shot. Three trucks full of German soldiers to capture two Jewish girls. They amplify visibility, they amplify sound, they thrive on terror. Visibility is so central in capturing us—for the purpose of making us invisible.

Gestapo Prison. A dark, damp cell. Mirjam and I are the only ones in it. There are others in other cells. Straw in the corner, a bare light bulb. There is writing on the wall—names and messages in several languages, some in Hebrew lettering.

### Your years a tale

I recognize you
who passed through
and left your marks
on these prison walls

Your years a tale
of harmonica sounds
of planted corn
mended shoes

you carried little ones
across the brook
you prayed — you whistled
fixed the roofs and lit the lamps

made bread — made wine
danced and teased
drank buttermilk
fear not, fear not

may these walls rot
ere I forget your
years your tales


. . .


You who come here
after me recount
my tale my years
my brevity


By now everyone has heard of Gestapo interrogations. Even in this
universe of terror there are gradations. The Gestapo, whose spe-
cialty is interrogation, has the reputation for the worst torture. I
know the story of Mr. Berger, a family friend. He is interrogated
by the Gestapo. Interrogated and tortured. During one such torture session, the interrogator keeps asking him, "What do you say?"
Whatever his response, the torturer continues the beating and
repeats, "What do you say?" Finally a local policeman whispers in
his ear, "*Povedz dakujem*"—say thank you. He does and is thrown
back into his cell where he dies. His family is allowed to bury him.
Later Gestapo victims have no family to bury them. They are already
deported. I know of other Gestapo stories as well and my fear is
commensurate. I am terrified. Mirjam less so. She knows less.

A guard takes me into the interrogation room. They want to
know where my family is hiding. Where other Jews are hiding. I
will be released if I tell. They say Mirjam already informed. They
lie, neither of us knows of these hiding places. They threaten and
yell, and I persist I do not know. I am pushed around, but not
beaten, though the rod is always in their hands. With Mirjam they
alternate. She is promised chocolate in return for information, or
she is yelled at and threatened.

"*Nehm ja den Kuchen. Sehr frisch.*" The young Gestapo man
coming towards us is offering poppy seed cake from the large

platter he is carrying. "*Danke.Gerne.*" My guard takes two slices. Pushing me ahead, he and I continue to the interrogation room and the cake carrier on to his pleasant task.

Do they not see me during this interaction? I feel invisible, worse—blotted out. Irrelevant. Had they at least indicated a moment of discomfort on my behalf—a recognition that another human was present! I want the cake, my favorite, but do not expect it. But intensely, cravingly, I want some acknowledgment of my presence during this interaction. I want deliberate, intentional ignoring, a sign that I exist. This brief experience fills me with the dread of negation.

During this interrogation, I almost wish I had the information they are after... so I could defy them by withholding it. They sense my increased resistance. They get tougher.

The interrogations continue for days—always separately. They demand to know with such entitlement, no allowance is made for reluctance to betray a parent, a friend. Fortunate in our ignorance... our ignorance rather than bravery prevents disclosure.

Daily diet is stale bread, watery porridge, and water. We are more scared than hungry.

"Don't make a sound and follow me," whispers a Slovak policeman during the night. He leads us out through a side door and instructs us to run to a waiting car nearby. The driver takes us to Stara Lubovna, a town nearby where relatives are in hiding.

Another Christian family takes in Mirjam. Mr. Lavka, a known anti-Nazi, is himself in hiding. The police come to the house frequently to search for him. The full ashtrays and opened cigarette packets left around the house at all times are a precaution—in case the police come the morning after one of Mr. Lavka's furtive visits. Son Rudo takes up smoking to disguise father's tobacco smell in the house.

When Mirjam hears the soldiers or police coming, she hides under the bed. They invariably find her. Then Mrs. L. explains, "My little niece is afraid of soldiers and hides."

Mirjam develops a high fever. Only a German doctor can be found. The family is in conflict. Should they risk her dying or risk betrayal? The doctor is called in. The diagnosis is scarlet fever. The family believes he suspects that Mirjam is Jewish, but he treats her, and she is not reported. The threatening unknown. The mistrust of goodness.

### Mirjam's Letter From Hiding

Why does this woman brush my hair
and make my braids so tight?
That brush is wrong!
I need my purple one
from home

Here — I should not be
my second grade is missing me

I like the dog
him I told
my birthday came
and no one called

All my life — and all the time
I have this name that's really mine
Now hear this — Mirjam — it — is!
Mirjam, Mirjam, Mirjam — is me!
But she says "child, Maria, it must be."

They say I cannot go outside to play
I may forget who I am not —
it is not wise — too great a risk
for a Jewish child to play outside,
that — I do not understand
I do not want to understand!
I want to go outside and play

but here I must do what others say!

I hate that here I cannot do
what at home I hate to do —
walk the dog — get up for school
wear dresses, hats to services
eat peas and beans before dessert

The mail in your vicinity
was stopped by some authority
no matter,
I have a plan that is much better.
(and besides
I have no paper
on which to write)

I will send this letter through my brain
and you will get it right away
Come and get me — I am ready
bring my doll, the orange ribbons
cookies in a special box
the woman might like that
quite a lot

P.S. I'll have to hide
when you ring the bell
but I will know you
I will know you
by your smell.

Mirjam's mother does not come. Mirjam survives thanks to this
"woman."

**Whom do you see?** There is a lull in deportations. I remain in Stara Lubovna in semi hiding, but move about more freely. Anyu is in Sered, a transit camp in Western Slovakia. From here transports are sent "East." Where "East" is we still do not know. I want to see her and plan to go there by myself. Aunt Irenke insists on accompanying me. The journey is many hours long. Jews are not allowed to travel, by public or private transportation. Irenke and I leave our yellow stars behind and travel as Christians. But we have no papers to back our claim. We are living on the edge, in hiding or in public. But I want to see Anyu. Identification by document is mandatory. We have none. We prepare an oral story if questioned.

Our story: Irenke is my aunt, my mother's sister. I visited her during my school vacation and she is taking me back home. "Home" would be the city nearest to the station at which we may be questioned. We would then get off at the next stop. Therefore , we memorize several places along the route.

Police and soldiers patrol the railway platform. They look relaxed, are not checking papers. At any rate, turning back now would draw attention. Above all we must not draw attention.

Invisibility—we pray for invisibility. The soldiers and guards on the train appear equally relaxed. How confident they are that no Jew would dare defile their train. Other trains are reserved for Jewish travel. Other trains, other destinations. By now most Jews have already been deported.

Irenke and I look like other passengers. She is a pretty woman with dark hair. I am a girl with light hair in braids. We look like others and behave as they do—normally. Say, *"dobry dén"*—good day, smile at the child across, unwrap our bread and salami. Outward normalcy—internal terror. This travel is even more stressful and complicated. than hiding. The Jew in hiding is a Jew fearing discovery. On this train a Jew hiding behind the mask of the non-Jew role is living both roles with terrifying intensity. What others do with ease, we do with trepidation. Exhausting to be a Christian.

The train stops, we get off to buy refreshments. There are kiosks on the platform, and sellers cry out their wares. We buy drinks, hot dogs, and chocolate. Upon return we find others in our seats. A young boy and a woman with an infant in her arms. Paralyzing indecision, how do we deal with this situation? Do we act like people with paid up tickets and rights, or do we minimize our visibility—not rock the boat? What would "normals" do? Other passengers are watching. Irenke decides in favor of civility—accommodation. She smiles at the infant and tells the woman to remain seated. (That woman does not in the least look inclined to move!) Irenke then hands me our bags from the overhead rack. We find seats in the next compartment. A minor inconvenience for "normals," a life and death issue for us.

This journey demands other decisions as well. Do we go to the bathroom one at a time or together? What if there is an identity check during our separation? We decide on separate. The family injunction holds here too—whoever can, must—survive.

Should we engage in conversation with other passengers or feign sleep? We decide on friendly—but tired. I take my cues from Irenke, unspoken cues.

I would like this journey under other circumstances. Trains are fun. Irenke is at all times good company. Pleasing to look at, people always look at her. She welcomes that. She is generous, tells me things, asks my opinion. I have traveled with her on many vacations. Irenke enhances.

The lovely scenery is what brings the tourists to this part of the country. Before the division of the country, when Slovakia became an ally of Hitler, we used to sing the Czech national anthem in school. The gentle anthem celebrating the lovely scenery we are now passing.

## Where is My Home?

Where is my home, where is my home?
Streams are rushing through the meadows,

Scene of Tatry Mountains in Slovakia. Photo by author.

'Mid the rocks sigh fragrant pine groves.
Orchards decked in spring's array
Scenes of paradise portray.
And this land of wond'rous beauty
Is the Czech land, home of mine,
Is the Czech land, home of mine.

This anthem is now forbidden. The Slovak one is harsher, more nationalistic. I am not too distressed that Jews are not allowed to sing it.

We also learned haunting poems about men transporting wooden logs on these harsh rivers and of the women waiting for their return—silently waiting. Poems about nature. Dramatic, intense poems.

Opposite me sits a woman dressed in local native costume with a basket in her lap. Next to her sits a nun in black habit. I am wearing my red sandals and print cotton dress and reading a book about a country girl attending a convent school. My mother went to a convent school; the quality of education there was better than in the public school. I cannot share this information with the nun, cannot risk inadvertently revealing dangerous truths. I hope these women don't probe beyond my sandals and book.

The peasant woman opens the basket and unfolds a white embroidered cloth. She offers the nun a pear and homemade bun and then, smiling, the same to me. Irenke's eyes are closed. Perhaps she really is asleep, deception is exhausting. The nun and I accept. The nun crosses herself and then eats.

What do I do? Is there a blessing before eating—like there was at home? I do not know from which direction to start making the cross. We did not prepare for such an eventuality. During hiding I learned the Lord's Prayer—just in case—but not the movement of the cross. I put the pear and bun into Irenke's bag, and pointing at her dutifully, say that I will share these with my aunt when she wakes up.

"*Dobre devcatko*"—good girl—the woman says, and the nun nods approvingly.

What if they knew?

What if they knew that this red-sandaled girl is risking her life to see her mother one more time? Her mother, who is alone, sick, and about to be deported. That her aunt is endangering her own life to help. That a fifth generation family of this land is denied citizenship, home, safety, options, life. That her nine-year-old brother is hiding in the woods, and half the lifetime of her seven-year-old sister is spent escaping, imprisoned, hiding, fearing. That her father in a labor camp is forced to pick tobacco for the German army.

You people on this train, whom do you see?

I am lucky they see the faked me.

We are allowed to visit Anyu in the camp hospital. She looks so thin. She introduces me to the nurses on the floor. I sit on the bed and hold her hand. Time to leave. I do not see her again. She dies that summer in that Lager. A letter arrives from father. He writes, "And now I have only you children." He does not say Anyu died. The implication is clear, but I pretend it is not so. I do not mourn. I need her alive, because my own motivation to stay alive is fully connected with the need "to tell Anyu." That and caring for Mirjam and Karpu.

**Deportations resume.** Everyone, no exemptions. Their plan remains unchanged. Ours too. We will continue to defy their plan.

Elza, Mella, Mirjam to stay in hiding. Apu and Moshe are in a labor camp in Slovakia. They are needed there, but plan to escape if deportations threaten. Frieda and family are somewhere in hiding. For the rest of us the only available option is the forest. Aunt Irenke, Yidu, and Karpu will go to a cabin in the woods, together with her aged parents. I think it very unfair that she be responsible for the most vulnerable family members and offer to go with her. She insists that I cannot help and must go with Ella's group. Aunt Ella and Noach, her husband, agree to take me along. Yossi, their teenaged son also joins them.

Is this wood deep enough
dark enough
far enough
to hide me?

**In the forest.** We walk for several days to reach the depth of the forest. The group of about fifteen men and women is on the move. Occasionally we sleep in some hunting cabin or shepherd's hut, but mostly outdoors. Always fully clothed. Clara, dressed in peasant clothing, buys food in nearby villages—black bread, potatoes, raw bacon. When food is short we eat berries from the forest. How many centuries ago did I refuse non-Kosher food? Centuries now measured in months, days, less...

The occasional news we get from the outside is good. The Allies are advancing in Europe, the Russians in Poland. "So how much longer can this war last?" our oft repeated optimistic refrain.

I fantasize the after...

## Unhiding in the Forest

When war is done
I will metamorphosize
into visibility
I'll wear scarlet
I'll make noises
invite echoes

bonfires and picnic baskets
I'll bring along a friend
or two or three or seventy

I'll leave the berries
to the birds
I will not fear
your din of thrush or brush
nor fear
lest a human should appear

trees dense or sparse
what's it to me?
I'll be cloaked in visibility!
hang in there
wait for me
and I will do my best
to be

How much longer can this war last? A long time longer.

## Judith in Hiding

Does it make sense — to be wet and cold
with so much wood all around?

NO FIRE — no fire — by night or day
a fire in this place would give you away!
the berries we pick are good as a treat
but meal after meal — and day after day

my teeth protest — "No More — No More
No More — of that!"

I do not complain, no one does
would that be of use to us?

we plan and we guess which way to go
due South or due North — later or now ?

do we stay with the groups — or split up in twos ?
the wrong answer — means disaster

so out in that forest — under that sky
there isn't a route that we do not try

*"Get up! Mach schnell — you dirty Jews!"*
the soldiers appear — with dogs and guns
those of us who try to run — are chased and shot
the chase is pleasing to the dogs.

we are marched to the trucks — we travel light
all we have we leave behind.

in prison now — the dogs are fed
the dogs did fine — the forest now is Judenrein

"Raus! Raus! Schnell!" Once again I wake with a gun and bayonet pointing at me. This night we sleep on the floor of a hut. German soldiers fill the hut. The forest. The universe. They and their dogs. At gunpoint they push us outside. Hanni asks, "Can I take my coat?" The soldier hits her on the head with a gun. She collapses and some-one helps her out. A man from our group starts to run uphill. He is shot in the back. His wife runs towards him; she is also shot. (Their infant daughter is with a farm family whom they pay. When the family hears of the death of the couple, they poison the baby.)

So many soldiers for so few of us. They are always in a hurry to get us there... This is the first time I see a man shot, a woman shot.

Shot is not a word, not a scene on a photograph. Shot is a stranger barely moving a finger, and our friend stumbles like a drunken wedding guest, then lies on the forest ground face down-ward. We do not see István's face but I know his last bit of life was of surprise. (Was... already was?) István was a very planful man—he planned our daily moves. He planned his infant daugh-ter's safety. He did not plan to be shot in the back, uphill. Wife Roszie trusted his planning. She followed his every move.

They give us no time to register this terror. Rifle-butted into waiting trucks we are driven out of the forest. What happened to the couple—their bodies? Who will bury them? Where? I am still thinking of individual burials. Not mass graves. Not no graves.

They come with dogs. They come with guns. Trucks. In large numbers. Do they not feel ridiculous with this outsized might, this over-poweredness? Is this glory?

God, how are we so visible to them and so invisible to You? You owe us visibility—

Yours.

# Chapter Four

# Prison

This prison in Kezmarok is a converted castle. *"Du kommst mit mir."* The soldier grabs Vera by the hair. She says, *"Wohin?"* *"Schweig, Jude!"* He pushes her towards the door.

Vera is a fashion model. She is tall, green-eyed with fair wavy hair. We all like her because she is so approachable, helpful, and tells good jokes. Bundi, her boyfriend, watches over her, and we secretly smile at his "overprotectiveness," especially when she gives him that "I can take care of myself" smirk. But now she cannot, and Bundi, who moves toward her, is forcefully thrown against the wall. He gets up and again moves towards her; the soldier grins and says, *"Na, komm ja auch mit."* Well, come along then.

Vera is tortured in front of Bundi. She and Bundi are both shot the following day.

We are taken individually into a room and body searched for valuables. The officer in charge is not SS, the elite guards of the Nazi Party, he is from the Wehrmacht Division. Handsome, polite. *"Hast du Schmuck oder Geld?"* Do you have jewelry or money? I should hand it over, I will not be punished. He can understand that the adults would give me their valuables to hide. I need not fear. Nothing will happen to me, he states reassuringly.

*"Ich habe nichts."* I have nothing, I tell him; we handed all in while I was still at home. He orders me to undress and another soldier checks my clothing. Then my naked body is searched. The officer keeps an eye on me throughout. Finally, he asks, "Was your father or mother German?"

"Neither," I say. "I am Jewish."

He exclaims, *"Ummöglich—du bist ja so rein."* Impossible, you are so clean.

Later I hate myself for being flattered by his comment, but would it be so bad not to be a "dirty Jew" right now?

When we are eventually moved into a large hall and given bread and warm soup, I notice how fit and clean some prisoners look. They must have come straight from home, not from attics or forests. I become an expert at identifying prisoner contexts—when last washed with soap, when last eaten cooked food, when stopped praying. True, my assumptions are never tested.

The day after our capture my brother Karpu is brought in. He, cousin Yidu, Aunt Irenke, and her parents are found in another part of the forest. Karpu and Yidu are nine and Irenke's parents almost eighty. It is such a sad event, but I am so happy to see them. My sweet impish brother, my favorite aunt, Yidu. Yidu, dark haired with sparkling brown eyes, looks the opposite of fair-haired, blue-eyed Karpu. The boys belong together. But not here! And not here the grandparents. The grandparents need a warm bed and warm tea. None of us should be here, but especially not them. We must get them all out of here. The next day they are all sent to Auschwitz, and I never see them again. And I never... I never not think about how they did in the wagon train? How did Irenke hold all their hands? Of such questions are my nightmares.

### Karpu in Auschwitz

eight — perhaps as much as nine
I teased him around our kitchen table.

Did anyone want to
care to
was strong enough to
touch his pale hair
when gas was filling?
and his breathing
his breathing
I want to be there
and help him breathe
and postpone dying
and I do not want
to die
until he does
and — and —

My brother will forever be nine.

**Presov prison.** For our group another prison in another town, this a Gestapo prison. Uncle Noach and Aunt Ella sit on the cell floor leaning against the damp stone-wall. Yossi is flirting with a long-haired girl. Sparse straw covers the bare floor. I sit next to Ella. The two of them talk quietly discussing escape plans.

Noach: "If I can get a message out to Judge R., he will get us out of here."

Ella: "What is in it for him? You are in prison with nothing."

Noach, intensely: "Precisely, he will know that I want out and that I can make it worth his while. He knows he will be well rewarded."

Ella: "It would be safer to send a message to him through his butcher. His maid shops there every morning." They know this town. They lived here for a while.

Soon Noach goes to the small barred window of the metal door and calls out. He tells the guard something and hands him a small wrapped package. The guard nods, takes it, and moves away. A minute letter he opens the door, looks around the crowded cell, and when he spots Noach, motions him towards the door. When Noach stands in front of him, the guard raises his hand and hits him full force on the face. Then again. Full might. Noach's nose is bleeding. The guard spits and says in a raging voice, "*Ins Feuer, Jude!*" Into the oven, Jew! He leaves, slamming the door shut behind him.

Yossi jumps up and rushes for the door. Several men restrain him. No one doubts Yossi would kill the guard regardless of consequences. And this time no one would say Yossi is so impulsive. This time all would understand. This time all are relieved that Yossi is restrained. Justifiable action is not for Gestapo prisons.

Ella, pale and scared, is helping Noach back to the straw seat by the wall. No one asks him any questions, and he does not offer explanations. Soon his face is swollen and his nose continues to bleed. Some crumpled handkerchiefs are passed along to serve as bandages. How did Noach manage to hide the gift he tried to bribe the guard with? That thorough German search in Kezmarock seemed so foolproof to me.

Noach says to Ella through swollen lips, "Someone must have seen that guard accept the ring. He was probably protecting himself by beating me."

Ella pleading, "Noach, please don't try anything else. They will be watching you closely."

He nods unconvincingly, and she knows her husband is unable not to try again. I go back and forth rinsing the bloodied handkerchiefs in the dirty water from the pail in the corner. Noach looks bruised, but not defeated. Ella looks beaten. Noach always acts as though setbacks are just an unpleasant detour along the way.

I have been in this prison before—with Mirjam, brought here after our capture from hiding. You can tell a Gestapo prison immediately. All is harshness. Violence permeates all. Even when they do not torture you, you imagine it. Even if the pain is not in your body, it is in your head. The possibility clutches. I am terrified of physical violence...let it not be...let it not be...let it not be...in the body. And all of me is poised to live.

We are fortunate. No interrogation. They know enough. They strut with the same harsh, arrogant certainty when they do not want to know as when they do want to know. All the certainty is on their side. Never doubts. What is their agenda for today? They do not tell. Uncertainty is part of their torture. By now any one of us can contribute to rumor making. We fill the void by conjecturing. We will be shot as punishment for the attempt on Hitler's life—though Jews were clearly not involved in that. So? Germany needs workers; we will be sent to work in factories. Overseas Jewish organizations will arrange to trade us for trucks.

We are not abused, just deprived. We cannot leave the cell and our food looks and tastes like warmed over animal fodder—in the morning and at night. Some days we get bread and tea at noon. More of the flop is eaten on day two and still more on subsequent days. We are getting used to it. Getting "used to" is becoming a lifestyle.

The cell smells of urine and mildew and our unwashed bodies.

The dirty pail, tin cup next to it. Names written all over the damp stonewalls. Written in pen and pencil, scratched in, and I, the recidivist, recognize prisoner commonality. Recognize the desire of the prisoner of every cell, of every time, to leave a mark...a person with a name passed through here.

> I recognize you
> who passed through
> and left your marks
> on these prison walls
> Your years a tale...

Noach is unable to eat. Ella feeds him tea.

Obviously you, Germans, do not want to see a prisoner save himself. But is it an affront to you that a prisoner would want to?

Stupid men! Do you expect us to accept your agenda for us as passionately as you do? Willingly consent? See us through our eyes!

I am passive in my outward resistance—in standing up to them directly. Torture terrifies me so. I resist by hiding, escaping, impersonating. But I am with Noach in wanting to live. I taste his determination. And Yossi's. It is impossible to imagine Yossi out of existence. He exists in every pore.

### Such good taste

I overheard
Hauptmann Kurt
say to
Kapitän Schmidt
"Liesel will like
this gold watch
she has such
good taste.
Die Jüdin
wanted water in
return.
Stupid swine
always water
always asking!"

**Wagon train.** The platform is crowded with Jews—fenced in by cattle cars in front and a wall of SS men behind—with dogs. Some people carrying bundles or suitcases are slow to climb onto the wagons. They are speeded along with rifle butts. Soon some young Jewish men stand by the entrance of the wagon and help the people up. Their task gets more difficult as the wagon gets more crowded. They now have to push people into the back to

make room for more. More. More. These men, who start out to
help their fellow Jews are involuntarily transformed into SS aids,
aiding the process of making the territory Judenrein.

Does this brutal induction allow them no time to consider their
new role? Do they decide that their pushing is more humane than
rifle butts and bayonets? They brutalize us with choiceless choices.

The doors are noisily bolted from outside. Over one hundred
of us in the space meant for eight horses and no people, but which
could probably accommodate forty people. Noach quickly takes
a seat by the wall and pulls Ella down next to him. Yossi waves from
the opposite wall. He sits next to the long-haired girl. I sit in front
of Ella, knees pulled up. There is no room to stretch my legs out.
Those standing have no room to sit. The pail in the middle, serving as toilet, is empty for some time. Social inhibitions still oper-
ate. Then the pail is quickly filled. There is no lid. It spills over, and
those nearby cannot move away. Soon, none can escape the smell.

There are bars on the only small window near the ceiling.
A discussion ensues. Should the bars be removed? Can they be?
Miraculously, some tools appear. Several nail files and one small
metal file. The discussion becomes quite intense on the subject
of escape.

"Yes—what can we lose?"

"No. It will endanger the rest of us. We will be shot as hostages."

The bars are removed. One man climbs onto the shoulder of
another and prepares to jump. He has red hair. The window is very
small, and he takes some time to push through it. Finally he takes
off his jacket and asks a man to throw it out after him. Then he
jumps. Immediately we hear a train rushing by from the opposite
direction. Nothing is said, and no one else jumps.

I notice the red-haired man does not say good-bye to anyone before jumping. That must have made his decision easier.
At times connections help and at times they complicate. But not
having anyone to say goodbye to surely means he said goodbye
already, along the way, somewhere. To whom? Where?

A mother and daughter sit near me. A young man keeps looking and smiling at the daughter. He finally reaches over and strokes her hair.

"You are pretty. What beautiful hair you have."

"Thank you," the girl smiles, pleased.

The mother says, "But when they cut her hair off in Auschwitz, will you still think her pretty?"

The girl pales and impulsively puts her hands onto her head, protecting her crown. She keeps them there until our arrival several days later.

What does the mother know about Auschwitz?

I do not know any specifics, only that Auschwitz is not a good place. Though I occupy only a small amount of space, my body is still too much for it. My body is in my way. When my legs are stretched out someone sits on them, When I pull up my knees I feel cramps. I cannot reach the bucket to urinate. My bladder is full, my stomach empty. And all of me craves water. I can no longer visualize water but am consumed by its absence. For periods my mind feels numb, then parched, then hot. Then, I do not know anymore. It is the third day into our journey. The train stops several times, but the doors are not opened. Banging from within: *"Wasser, Luft, Essen!"* Water, air, food. Response from outside: *"Schweig, Jude! Nicht für dich. Es gibt nichts."* Shut up, Jew! Not for you.

I fall asleep and wake in the same position, knees into my chest. Sleep provides some respite, but the physical constriction remains.

Still not given food, and worse yet, no water. Some people go mad, and there is no energy to calm or reassure them. Hallucinations get louder, pained silences meaner.

### Where my image?

too high
too small
too barred too walled

this window of
the wagon train

no air
no room
no space
for rage

look in, Lord
and for the record
record
(indelibly —
stone tablets
break so easily)

"I am your God,
your only God
in My image
created I, you
that you may
serve —

I seek My image
My image
where My image?"
Lord, what of
those who bolt
these doors?
seek You there
the Holy sphere ?

Day four. Doors are noisily unlatched. We push to get out to the
field across the platform with the buckets of water. Thirst. The
numbed, the crazed, the parched, propelled into motion. We cup

the water into our hands and drink and gulp and drink. Few available tin cans get passed around. Water cannot be taken back into the wagon train, but at the entrance each is given a loaf of bread. Those who went mad recover. Now only the situation is mad. I comfort the little boy while his mother tries to calm his younger brother. Someone passes chocolate to the children—joy and then thirst.

On the fifth day the train stops again. The doors are not opened. We wait...I know it is the fifth day by the five scratched lines on the brown wagon wall. The man on the floor next to me marks the days with a pin of a small brooch. He makes his daily marks when daylight enters the small window. Shimon, a partisan with the Slovak National Resistance movement, is one of the few resisters not shot when caught.

Shimon handles the brooch all day but says nothing about it. I wonder about the brooch. Is it his girlfriend's—was she shot? Is it his mother's—where is she? His sister's? Questions I cannot ask, and answers I dare not hear. On a very basic level I want to know how he manages to keep the brooch in spite of the inevitable body searches?

Aunt Ella and Uncle Noach never mention their son, Ben. When they are not planning escape, when they are silent, I think they are thinking of Ben. Ben was deported when he should not have been. They were taking sixteen-year-olds; Ben was only fifteen and a half, so he was not hidden. Noach never felt more powerless and defeated than when he could not get his son out of prison.

Where are we going? What is Auschwitz? I know we do not want to go "East" to Auschwitz. I know that would be bad. When I am not so thirsty, I pray a lot and make a deal with God. "God, if we are spared Auschwitz, I will—after the war I will..." I make a promise God is sure to like.

We arrive in Auschwitz.

Under normal circumstances this journey should take less than a day. Under normal circumstances this journey should not be.

The door is unlatched. Yelling—"Raus, Schnell. Macht Schnell." Get out, get out. Hurry out. Leave all belongings on the train. "*Raus! Raus! Raus!*" Some orders are in Yiddish spoken by men in striped loose pajamas. They wear striped caps, stars, and have numbers above the stars. Are they also helping the SS? One striped man carries an old man out of the wagon. An SS guard kicks him, and he drops the man. "Throw him out. Don't carry him!" I realize the behavior of the striped helpers is forced upon them, but the old man...the old man...his daughter runs after him, screaming, "Don't step on my father. Don't! Don't!"

Chaos on the platform. People try to hold on to children, spouses, friends. It is dawn. After being rushed and shoved and beaten, we now stand and wait on the platform. From here we see multitudes. Masses of people, with no end in sight. There is dark movement, like ocean waves. What lies behind them? The striped prisoners are throwing luggage out of the train, but no one is allowed to claim it. Then, suddenly, their action is reversed and the luggage is thrown back in.

An announcement over the loudspeaker in German—"The transport on the platform is to go back into the wagons." A striped man whispers to my aunt in Yiddish, "*Sie hoben Glick—alles ist besser vie du.*" You are lucky. Anywhere is better than here.

There is a little more space inside the wagon. I can stretch my legs and keep them stretched. I comment on this to Ella.

She says, "The dead have been removed, so there is room for your legs."

"What? What did you say? How many died?" I shout, and pull my legs up. Ella says nothing. How do they know if they are really dead? Do people die so quickly? So quickly, without high fever, without protest?

We go on to Ravensbrück Concentration Camp, Germany.

Later we learn that because of the massive Hungarian deportations, even Auschwitz has no room for more Jews. Ten thousand people are gassed in a day during this time. We learn that we are the only transport to be sent on intact from Auschwitz.

Every survivor has a miracle story. Mine—no room in Auschwitz for that one day. How many trainloads were killed for that miracle? I do not know. I do not want to know.

> Are You not tempted,
> Lord,
> to intervene
> lend a hand
> prevent a scream?

# Chapter Five

## Ravensbrück

### Arbeit macht frei

In iron soldered certainty
ARBEIT MACHT FREI
proclaims the sign
above the Lager gate

Inside the gate
Herr Himmler's law —
work them as much
as possible
feed them as little
as possible
then let them die
replacements follow

Vernichtung durch Arbeit
replacements follow
frei to die

Their welcoming sign of "Work Makes You Free" is in fact a sentence of "Annihilation Through Work."

**Journey to Ravensbrück.** This journey from Auschwitz to Ravensbrück is shorter than the earlier part from Czechoslovakia to Auschwitz. That part was long. It is not shorter in kilometers, only in time. The train does not stop as often. The wagon is not as crowded; the dead have been removed. Now people do not go mad for lack of water. The thirst is not so intense. All else is. We now have the experience of an "Auschwitz arrival." This journey, though more physically tolerable, outdoes the terror of that earlier boxcar trip.

We feel more vulnerable. At that train station in Auschwitz we are confronted by something bizarre—we do not know the details, we do not know the facts, but we do know that this unreality is real. Those prior rumors now seem more ominous. We have seen guns, dogs, SS before. In Auschwitz all is amplified and so is our confusion and fear. The brutality is harsher. The multitudes in Auschwitz—dark continuous movement to where? How did so many get there? What lies beyond?

We now feel more vulnerable. We now have a precedent of what our next stop may be, though we still do not know fully what the last one was. We do not yet know about gas chambers. It is quiet in the wagon train. There is numbness. Families crouch together. Aunt Ella and Uncle Noach whispering, still planning escape. Will it suffice, their pooled resources? Ella's practicality, Noach's wheeling and dealing skill, Yossi's irrepressible zest and energy? Will it do? And my "resistance" stance? Will it suffice?

I think of death. How does a bullet feel? Will I know when to fall? Who will be next to me? Death by dog bite? I have seen a young boy attacked by a dog in Auschwitz—he was running after his father.

### I know a dog

I know a dog
I named him Ben
I named him Ben
when I was ten.

Oh, I could tell a lot
about that dog — but take my word
when you encounter him
you grin and grin.

I know a dog
his name is Hund
his master
with whip and gun
only
lets this big dog run
to kill and maim
and snare and bite
those of us
who are still alive

— he does not falter
this brute extension
of his master,
to encounter him
is grim, so grim.

I give up on that. On death. I cannot connect death with me. It's
domain is with the very old, the very sick. I am fourteen. I think
of home. I would like to be with my mother. I never am anymore.
So much to tell her.

I am hungry. I now know—from experience—on this journey hunger is followed by more hunger, as violent words are followed by violent acts. I am learning things I do not want to
know—I am experiencing what should not be.

It cannot be, I say, and am hit by a new evil, more terror,
and I am still at the stage of being surprised by every new brutality. How can this be, I still say. "How can this be" is why people around me are in shock. Numbed. Uncomprehending, we

react—but our reactions are for the world of "before"; they do not fit here.

A thirsty woman asking for water. She is hit with a rifle butt.

An infant crying—the mother offers her breast. The breast is empty.

A husband rushing to pull his wife away from an attacking German Shepherd. The man is shot.

A thirsty hand held out through the small window of the wagon train for rainwater is soon withdrawn, dripping blood.

Our life-directed movements are barred. How can this be?

The woman in this wagon train sits next to her boy. He is about eleven. He keeps pulling at his coat button and she reprimands, "Pauli, you will not look good with that button missing." Pauli continues—and the woman continues.

God, did you save that button? For eternity? Is there a more important act in Your universe than this mother trying to protect her child?

**Arrival.** Shrubs and greenery surround the railroad station of Fürstenberg. Vacation pretty scenery. Herded from the train onto trucks, we are driven through pleasant countryside of pine forests, neat houses, a lake. A big metal gate is opened by uniformed guards. Above the gate in huge iron letters the sign "*Arbeit Macht Frei*," work makes you free. From the gate, high brick walls stretch in both directions as far as you can see. The walls are topped with barbed wire. Inside the walls is an electric wire fence. Watchtowers surround these walls. Armed guards above us, armed guards with dogs around us. Minutes apart, this place inside the gate bears no resemblance to the outside. No trees, no green, no cottages. Flat barrenness.

Men and boys are separated from women. We never again see these men in Ravensbrück. Most of these men are not seen after Ravensbrück. Ella looks around for Noach and Yossi. They are lost

Felicie Mertens, "Die Walze" ("The Cement Roller"). Courtesy of
Sammlungen Ravensbrück.

in the crowd of marchers heading for the men's camp. Younger children stay with mothers. Since we are mainly a transport of Slovak
Jews, there are not many children in our transport. There are not
many left for transport. The Hungarians still have their children
to bring. Their deportations are more recent—spring, 1944. Ours
have been going on since 1942.

We sit outside with our belongings, of which I have none.
My life of late is weightless outside. Inside? Inside I do not know.
I cannot put the fragments together. After several cold hours
we are marched into a large hall but ordered to leave all belongings outside.

A lifetime of belongings reduced to a bundle and then less.
The clothing off our backs is soon taken as well. The contents—
flashlight, sweater, photographs, sewing kit, instant coffee, a mug,
a prayer book, a book, brush, house keys, socks—will be inte-
grated into the camp economy, or more likely confiscated for the

German Reich. Connections are severed. Severed from belongings, from people, from the known.

All night we sit, all night we wait, for information, for food, water, action. Questions asked of the women in stripes (we have met striped prisoners in Auschwitz, though those there were men) are not answered. Confusing—these striped uniformed women—some look fed and others emaciated. Some have hair, others are shorn.

What are those different colored triangles on their uniforms? Our questions are not answered. Some in stripes motion eyes toward the SS guards by the doors and all along the walls. Others respond with a kick or slap. We learn . . . no unsolicited communication is permitted. We are allowed to the lavatories, a few at a time, accompanied by the striped women. We sit all night and wait. As at the waters of Babylon—*al naarot Bavel*—we sit now and yearn for what was.

Suddenly orders are barked in German. No translation. All orders are in German, instant implementation demanded. Delay, hesitation, confusion—the whip, the scream, the slap. The language for us Slovak Jews is not as much of a problem as say for the French and Hungarians. Most of us speak German or Yiddish. The problem for us and for the Hungarians, Romanians, Poles—the problem for all of us—is how to become instant *Häftlinge*—prisoners. How do we shift into this universe where everything is different from what we know, from what we want to know? Nothing is familiar, yet we have to learn this ugly world instantly. Slow learning means punishment, means death. How can this be?

Some in the group are still drowsy. SS vocabulary awakens. Raus! Schnell! Whips! We are ordered to hand over valuables and money. Women in stripes, carrying baskets, accompanied by SS guards, walk past each row of new arrivals. Watches are handed over, a few rings. Lena, a young girl, is wrestling with her second earring—the SS guard rips it out leaving Lena with a bleeding ear and her mother screaming next to her. The guard drops the earrings into the pocket of her army uniform.

Orders. Undress completely for showers. Naked we wait, standing. I am learning the pattern. You wait dressed, undressed, standing, crouching. They are totally in charge. We are never, never allowed questions. Nazi communication. At moments of such extremes Aunt Ella and I glance at each other—"Are they for real—these obscene caricatures? What lies ahead?"

The room is cold and we stand naked—embarrassed still by each other's nakedness. An older woman holds a kerchief over her breasts, a guard snatches it and ties it around the woman's neck, tightening it . . . the woman's face turns red, purple, and the guard finally lets go. We all start breathing again—with the woman. With her, but we are not her. Only she knows the actual tightness around her neck. All coverings are now dropped unto the floor. Their method of ensuring obedience works. At every move they find opportunity for brutality.

As ordered, clothing is folded on the floor next to us. Shoes on top. A woman in stripes whispers to me in German, "Try and keep your clothes, your shoes—make sure your shoes." I am surprised to hear unaccented German from a prisoner. I am surprised to hear German that is not barked.

Because we are so crowded I manage to get into the shower room holding on to my clothes. Suddenly the striped woman appears and grabs my bundle of clothes from me. But why, I wonder, these will not fit her? She yells, "*Schnell, schnell!*" pointing to the showers.

Water comes in spurts—first too cold, then scorching hot, then nothing, then cold . . . we do not control the tap. No soap. No towel. No time. *Schnell. Schnell.* In over two weeks this is the first time I am able to wash, even though the water is cold and brown.

Is there a systematic schedule for this erratic water flow?

As I am nearing the door towards which we are now pushed, my bundle of clothes is thrust into my hands. Suddenly, I feel such incredible joy! To be reunited with something familiar—clothing from home. The striped woman disappears into the crowd, and I do not realize till later how often she saved my life by that gift of my own shoes.

## Shoes for life

I shall never not value shoes,
life is from the ground up
life with shoes
perhaps,
without — death

They know the value of shoes,
do they not keep the shoes
and dispose of the wearer?
No discrimination
— all sizes valued

"You will be shot instantly if any jewelry is found on you," by now an old refrain to me. I sleep in a bed and wear no yellow star when this order is first issued. They value valuables, lust for them.

Give us your gold, your rings, your cash
You greedy Jews have much of that!
(In my own mind I am confused
— is it not they who take from us
and take and grab and look for more?
And get real mad — when nothing more is to be had?)

So here goes one more "internal hygiene" examination. Naked, we wait over three hours for this examination. SS men always present. "Internal hygiene," another euphemism for the search for hidden gold and valuables.

We are in line for haircuts, head shaves that is. Soon those of us in back are ordered to *mach schnell*—get outside. Our hair is not cut because another transport is already waiting for processing. My hair is not cut. I am so relieved. The shaved heads look so shamed and unrecognizable. Finally something to be thankful for...my hair. Soon I have lice on my head...still...

The women with newly shaved heads do not recognize each other. Sisters search for siblings who are standing right next to them.

Male resemblances resulting from the head shaves bring the earlier separation from the men into the immediacy of the present.

Mother looking aghast at daughter: *"Istenem, hát te bátyád Péter vagy!"* My God, you are your brother Péter!—in Hungarian.

No mirrors. Women judge their own appearance by the appearance of others and hope they do not look like the others.

Another line—getting dark again—our second day here. Still naked and unfed. I do not put on my own clothing—I would be too conspicuous. Ella and a new friend from the transport, Hanicka, try to keep me between them as I carry my bundle. This line is for clothing.

Prisoners who arrive as women now emerge as men on top and scarecrows below. Some receive striped prison uniforms, invariably too long or too short. Others receive civilian clothing, stained and inappropriate. A black lace blouse and a skirt too tight to reach the waist. An evening gown or tennis shorts. The clothes are on a pile and the person next in line gets what is most handy to the distributor (a prisoner) who pays no attention to size or weather. No underwear is given. Nor are socks. Most women receive wooden clogs. A few get shoes that do not always match in color or size. Some get slippers and some high heels. Only a few minutes for this whole procedure. *Mach schnell! Raus!*—from the ever present SS guards. A request for a different dress, one that fits a little better, is met with slaps or kicks. SS are effective teachers. With each procedure we ask fewer questions, make fewer requests, fall into line faster. And we have been here less than forty-eight hours.... Once outside, some swapping takes place—furtively. Swapping is forbidden. But "furtively" is hopeful, they do not own us wholly.

Miraculously, I still have my hair, my shoes, my red polka-dot dress. (Miraculously? Is this what miracles are now made of?) In

Nina Jiriskova, "Trauernder Häftling—Mourning Prisoner." Courtesy of Sammlungen Ravensbrück.

this new order my hair, my shoes, my dress are not mine. By their law I am not entitled to what is mine. By their law it all belongs to the Third Reich. Aunt Ella has nothing from before. Aunt Ella is choicelessly law abiding.

God, do You notice? They reverse your Ten Commandments; they apply their own version to millions. Disposable millions. You shall not kill. You shall not covet. They kill and covet, kill and covet. Kill and covet.

Do You notice?

### Knew you then?

Before you knew
what now you do, before that
did you pat a cat?

wear summer shoes
before those boots?
bow before the Holy cross
ere you hailed the Haken Kreuz?
and did you throw a ball
tease a girl
practice how
to tie a tie
and help granddad
unknot the net?

that, before you crushed
the skull
of a sweet-haired child?

knew you then
the ways of men?
the ways of men
stead of the bloated
supermen?

be damned if you forgot
be double damned
if you did not

Evening of the next day and our induction still goes on. Dressed, we
are now lined up in rows and "categorized." Everyone in our group
is given two yellow triangles and two small pieces of cloth with a number—large and black. The triangles shaped into a star-of-David are
sewn onto our dress. The numbers, too, in duplicate, one above the
star, the other on the left sleeve. Now everyone can see I am prisoner:
"Jew number 83,621." Does this mean 83,620 women came here before
me? 83,621 women turned into numbers, and I see more coming even
as we stand here.

A woman in civilian clothing, clean and warm, with a green triangle, speaks to us in harshly accented German. It all adds up to numbers—you will be counted twice a day, you will be called by your number, not name, and you will be severely punished for any infraction. It is in your interest to obey.

Again, a line up of five—from now on group movement is always in fives—we are marched away. Numbered and nameless we enter the block (barrack). Ella and I take the upper of a three-tiered bunk. We have not been given food for two days, but more tired than hungry, we fall asleep ... in Ravensbrück, Germay, ninety kilometers from Berlin, the capital of the Third Reich.

**Magda.** In the bunk next to ours is Magda. She is from Hungary. Age twenty. Orders are in German. Magda does not speak German. Magda is at risk. She keeps repeating, *"Nem értem—nem értem."* I do not understand, not understand. She cringes at German, even when the words say "soup time." The harshness assaults her.

Magda, none of us understand, none of us, this is not understandable. But you must at least follow the rules. Though these are the least understandable ... they rule us to die.

### Magda speaks kein Deutsch

Magda speaks kein Deutsch
kein deutsch is not good
in this land of super-men
"Magda" I say, "do what I do —
line up for soup
— selections — de-lousing"
Magda into my shadow grows
— thinness amplified

"My friend " she says " here is my
bread
a gift for you for all you do."

A gift of bread — a gift of life
and more than that
a rest from hunger
that will not rest.

Two days later Magda lies
dead
I am relieved I made her keep
that gift of bread

(Oh, I do not lack for
choiceless-choice remembrances)

I do not shorten Magda's life
though I wish that I could have
a moment
full — of — bread

I give thanks daily that I do not take Magda's bread. Her death
would be on my conscience. But I can see trading my own life "for
a moment full of bread."

**Hunger.** Hunger in Ravensbrück is open-ended. There is no possibility of being sated, for closure, except through death. I am
never not hungry. Living time is hunger time. The day's focus
is on the evening bowl of thin soup and bread ration. Bread, but
not daily. The bread ration is about four inches wide. We hear
the bread is made up of flour and sawdust—I know of no one

Aat Breur, "Essen holen—The empty cauldron." Courtesy of Sammlungen Ravensbrück.

who rejects it on that basis. I systematically touch the spoon and bowl hanging from the rope around my waist.

### Hunger

First I make sure
I have my bowl and my spoon,

then, because soup time is still
beyond eternity's hill
with empty bowl
and spoon in hand
I practice eating, lest
— I forget.

You do not get soup without a bowl. The rope is bartered for two bread rations. Lost bowls are not replaced. Nothing is...

I examine the ground for something to chew on—grass, a plant, anything. There is nothing. All that grew was uprooted by others before me. Nothing that grew is replanted. Nature in here is on their side—it deprives and withholds. Change of seasons does not bring about change of barrenness.

Four more hours. Three. Soup is at six. The hours from four to six are the harshest. I develop a system of distractions...a different focus.

I will think of every thought I ever had.

I will think of every place I have ever been to.

I will think of every person I ever knew.

And then I think up new categories to move time along.

If someone is with me, I invite her to join my game. Most refuse. "Ein Kinder Spiel!" Kid stuff! I never play the game successfully. Hunger intrudes and grabs the foreground, but I try...try to subdue it with my own wishful agenda...

### Hunger do not intrude!

Hunger do not intrude
do not chagrin
do not shrill
do not presume
you are my all
you, you are

not my all
at all!

Hunger, note you this
— my Genesis,

Sun, be warm
be warm,Sun,
(hunger does not
let you in,
I am always shivering)

Crocuses, be purple pink.
bees, do not sting! Matching
buttons for my coat.
scratch that!
a new coat,
pale, pale grey,
a new comb for my
new hair

No barren soup
no turnips! No
black water!

A big book
hard covered
visible.

Sing birds
green songs, loud,
louder than all rifle shots.
gooseberry jam,
friends, cousins

(a boy in sandals
watches me
me, a hit? so be it!)

neighbor lady
look at me.
God Almighty
dance with me.

When I put on the yellow star, neighbors at home stop looking at me.

Pretending, imagining, is not easy here, reality intrudes and grabs. Hunger resists distraction.

Evening soup, thin water with potato peels, turnips, or beets. With great luck, a potato. The eating of soup is accompanied by the crunching of dirt or sand in the mouth. Is this the result of the unwashed rotten vegetables? Are these intentionally added ingredients? Sometimes we are given a slice of cheese or margarine. Occasionally, watery jam. Is the bread ration cut evenly? Will I get the potato from the bottom? Is it better to be in front or in back of the line? There are always favorites of the soup ladler. And sometimes I am favored.

After the soup, eaten with total concentration, in silence, the women in the bunks speak of recipes. How much butter for a cream cake, how much sugar, how much flour for strudel, chalah, torte? Each one's recipe is foolproof, well tested, been in the family forever. Some are willing to negotiate ingredients, others never. No talk of family back home, just food back home, easier. But family images come with the recipes. Baking was done with mother; father cut the challah. Baking smells warming winter mornings. Bertha laughing, "I cannot give you the exact recipe for stuffed cabbage, my mother-in-law shares her food, but not her recipe."

I am thinking of the half bread ration I am saving for morning to see me through Appell, roll call. Mostly my sensible plan fails. I eat the bread before lights go out at 9:00 p.m. The open-ended hunger continues, but for a while with less intensity.

Once I have a splendid dream. I am carrying lunch to the potato pickers in our field. Hot soup with vegetables. Noodles with cheese and poppy seeds. And rolls. As I am leaving, grandmother calls me back and adds pears to the basket. It all goes into the small wagon I pull to the fields. The pickers are waiting. They give me a baked potato hot from the open fire, still burning. They bring their own salt in linen handkerchiefs. When I awake to the nightmare of the roll call whistle, I tell Ella my dream. She envies me. Good dreams, like good realities, are hard to come by. Nightmares abound.

When we get here the camp is overcrowded. Conditions continue to deteriorate. Contrary to earlier rules, soup is now given only once a day instead of twice. The camp is no longer a detention place for the "re-education" of political prisoners. Now it is turned into a slave labor camp and annihilation place—*Vernichtungs Lager*—especially for Jews and Gypsies. Gas chambers have been introduced and are operating fully.

### The left shoe

The gypsy girl
has one shoe
the left shoe

Inside the shoe
an orange rag
right up to her knee,
formerly her right-hand
sleeve

Mutter? she asks
of every woman
in her path.
A hundred, a thousand, million
Mutter? Mutter? Mutter?

That gypsy child
never gets it
*right*

You left child, who will provide rightness for you? Who will call
your name?

**The Child.** Sometimes a woman "adopts" an orphaned child.
And sometimes a child finds no one to connect with. And sometimes children move about in small groups of their own. In this
part of the camp I see very few children. But I also see such ten-
derness between women and children for whom they care, or
try to. Anka tries. She "adopts" a little Czech girl. And one day
when we return from Appell, the little girl is gone. Even the brutal *Blockälteste,* the prisoner in charge of our barrack, does not
try to stop Anka's screaming. She probably knows it is safe, that
the SS are heading for comfort after the three-hour Appell.

Screaming is verboten, even for a "selected" child. Had the
Blockälteste intruded, I think this is the one instance where we all
would have turned on her. I hope we would have.

Our fury comes from Anka's pain. We allow it visibility because
we, too, know the SS are distant. This one time the Blockälteste
fears us. She withdraws into her room with her companion.

Is this victory, Anka loses her child, but she is allowed her
screams?

Stand still Sun
make dark the world

spotlight this site
of primal night
let wise men come
let wise men see

mother and child
mother no child

none or some
more or none

this inn does all accommodate
as ashen skies regurgitate.

Hungarian mother Shari slaps daughter Vera, "Just because I am
not here does not mean you can stop eating. Eat. Now. You are still
growing. Not later. Now." *Nem Késöbb. Mostan.*

Vera shelters three days of bread rations next to her bare chest.
Sleeps with the bread. Saves it for mother. Mother Shari is now back
in our block because Vera, with help from some friends, smuggles
her out of the block of "old women." Shari is forty-three. Vera rescues mother after she hears of the imminent selection there.
Punishment death. For Vera it is worth the risk.

The whole block is impressed. Death, be you also. Do not
intrude, let the rescue be. Let mother Shari fuss over her still
growing daughter. A small deprivation for you, infinity for
mother. Let it be.

**Pani Rakovska.** Pani R. and her teenaged daughter are in the bunk
behind ours. She wants to be addressed as Pani—Madam. Insists

Helen Ernst, "In Memoriam Lidice—In memory of the massacre of Lidice, Czechoslovakia." Courtesy of Museum Schwerin.

on formality. She must be what she claims to be—of the Polish aristocracy—for she has a needle, thread, and fabric and is sewing a coat for her daughter. I never see another needle or thread or fabric in this place. She tells in Polish of being related to a high-ranking SS official in Ravensbrück and expects to be released any day, that unlike us, she and daughter do not belong here. (We do?) There is no embarrassment or apology in her statement. Their imprisonment is a mistake. She is not anti-Nazi and is certainly not Jewish! I am envious of her claim to privilege and freedom. Even of her disdain toward us. With arrogant certainty she claims her birthright.

Unfair imprisonment? Mistaken imprisonment? Are there valid claims? Is there an arbitrator who listens?

I learn the ranking system of who may disdain whom. German political prisoners over German criminal prisoners—red over green triangles. Green over black triangles—black are prostitutes, a-socials, slackers, Gypsies. Poles over Russians. Everyone over yellow—over Jews. All we Jews have are Jews of other nationalities. Our rank superiority is insignificant. Rumor has it that Jehovah's Witnesses, lavender, elicit so much trust they are even allowed to shave the SS. They also work as maids in SS homes. They have a reputation of uncompromising faith and honesty. They are here because they refuse to acknowledge Hitler as their Führer. Refuse to make the "Heil Hitler" salute or swear allegiance to the Nazi State.

I am also envious of Pani R's stock of jam and cheese. Where does she get it? I believe her story, but the SS do not. Either they do they not believe her story or it is irrelevant to them.

They are good victim makers and their enormous net absorbs all, even aristocratic Pani R. and her daughter. To accommodate all, they establish hundreds of camps in Germany, Poland, Lithuania, Romania.

I ask Pani R. how she managed to present her case to them? She shakes her head irritably and does not say. Her teenage daughter does not respond to my overtures of friendship either. Because of our Slavic languages we could understand each other. Because of our different colored triangles, it was not to be. I could use a friend my age.

It must be hard for Pani R. to be a Nazi supporter from the inside of a Concentration Camp. But she remains steadfastly loyal and continues to hate Jews.

here I should not be
my friends out there
are missing me

Where out there? Who out there? My Jewish friends do not exist. To my Christian friends, I do not exist.

### Ravensbrück Heil

We fed you well
eyes, ears
shrunken breasts
empty thighs
— not much meat there
but always fresh
Heil, rats

**Washing: my resistance.** I at first run out of the washroom with the cold water taps because the floor is covered with bodies of naked women. I run outside. Two women are pulling a cart of naked bodies piled high on top of each other. I turn and look away.

"*Na, du weisst doch, die ist ja eine Neue!*" You can tell she is a new one, says one corpse carrier to the other.

I run out of the washroom with the coldwater taps . . . the naked bodies have no flesh on them. Skin covers only bones; there is nothing in between. Body parts are missing, eaten by rats. The living do not scare the rats away; they ignore us. The rats feed upon the dead, the lice upon the living. Ravensbrück harvest.

I go back in to wash. I step over the body near the washbasin and then three more bodies before I get to the water tap. There are more bodies along all the walls and in the center. The women in here died of starvation or illness. The women who are shot or beaten are usually left outside the block. The women who are "selected" are taken away live. Categories of dead. So many ways to die. How do I absorb such facts? Skin and bones will never be a cliché to me. Shrunken, hollow, gaping, rat eaten . . . never, never just words. How do I erase this, the enormity of this diminution, this shrunkenness?

God, where does this fit? This plague? This death of the first-born, the second-born, the all born . . .

No soap, and for towel a small handkerchief sized piece of cloth. Am I cleaner? The lice stay on. But opening the tap—in the midst of this horror—I feel somehow empowered. I am continuing the Kurima legacy, "We must survive. We must resist." I am hearing Anyu's injunction to take care of Karpu and Mirjam. I must live. Though there is not always water in the tap, I continue the routine of "washing."

And are we not commanded to wash hands before making the blessing before and after every meal? I skip the blessings, they skip my meals. But washing becomes my form of resistance. My defiance helps me, but I know that others, more determined, braver in their defiance, are dead.

Washing is my form of resistance. I want them punished for Mrs. Rheinhardt's resistance. I first see her in prison back in Czechoslovakia. There she wears a white blouse and I can tell, I can tell, she has till recently washed with warm water and soap and shampoo. And she has such dignity. In Ravensbrück, in my barrack, she shuffles very quickly into death. She does not try in any way to adapt. She will have none of it. One day, as we rush to Appell—roll call—she sits open-eyed on a chair. A prisoner running by shouts, "Appell time," and kicks the chair. Mrs Rheinhardt falls over. She is dead. Her resistance. She will not live in a world without dignity. I want them punished. For that I want them punished. Damn them for her choice! For giving herself over to death.

They should answer for her disconnection, for her discontinuity. See to it, world. God, demand accountability. Will that comfort Mrs. Rheinhardt?

When I come back from Appell there is a new mound of bodies in front of the block. I no longer look away. I do not recognize Mrs. Rheinhardt anymore. Here people's appearances change very quickly. Quickly, unrecognizable from haired to shaved, from nourished to starved. And when they are dead—edges and bones—no longer distinguishable. If their eyes are open, you wish they were not. Open eyes demand connection. Should I ever meet a member of Mrs. Rheinhard's family I will not tell details.

How will I tell Anyu, not just my own Ravensbrück stories, but all these other stories around me? I hold on to my pretense of Anyu being there for my stories. That is how it has to be.

Even if you have a bearable day there are always others who do not. Whose days, like Mrs. Rheinhardt's, are not bearable.

How much looking away can you do? Do you want to do? Where can you look? God, please do not make me immune to all. Do not make me immune.

**Aunt Ella.** Aunt Ella and I share a bunk. We are on top of this three-tiered wooden, shaky structure. Later, when the Hungarians and others come from Auschwitz and Buchenwald and Bergen Belsen and—we are four to a bunk and then more. Beds have to be made according to regulations, flat and neat. When we get even more crowded, rules are loosened. No sheets, of course. Lice. Bedbugs. A thin, stained blanket. One blanket per bunk. It is pulled in all directions. In the end warmth comes from the body next to yours, unless the body is dead.

I still have my own clothing. My red cotton polka-dot dress is not the most desirable camp attire, but it connects to "before." I do not have a change of underwear. Most people have no underwear. Or socks. I do not wash my dress or underwear. Where would I hang them? Who would guard them? Things left unguarded quickly disappear.

What would I wear in the meantime? I have no substitutes. The only place assigned for personal use is a third or a quarter of a bunk. But my shoes . . . my shoes. I owe them . . . life is from the ground up.

Ella has nothing, nothing from before. Because of the summers my cousins and I vacationed in her home, I know she likes "good quality" things.

Ella even had suits knitted for her—"they fit better." Her husband, Noach, made money and brought home fine watches. She loved her Omega watch. Swiss made. She paid much attention to her appearance. "Good cuts," for her thick, dark hair. Polished nails. Shoes—she chose her shoes with great care—fine, soft Italian leather, well stitched, the right shade to match her knitted outfits. And handbags too, she liked them "elegant." Channel #5 perfume. Noach, too, was a good dresser. His taste was more flashy. Subdued elegance, that was Ella.

Here, too, she focuses on appearance. Shortly after our arrival in Ravensbrück, she trades bread for rags—to wrap around her feet, now shod in wooden clogs. She does this for warmth and to prevent sores and blisters from the wooden clogs. She continues to trade, two or three bread rations for a rag.

With sore feet you shuffle. Shuffling is not keeping up on the march, slowing down at work, lateness for Appell. They shoot the slow, the late, the stumbling. Shuffling is death. They are obsessed with speed and fitness in this pit of unfitness. But no bread also slows you down. Ravensbrück choices. Ella chooses rags—yes, life is from the ground up.

Before Ravensbrück, she mourns for her son Ben. Ben who is deported in 1942 in an early transport "unjustly." They take him over Ella's pleading and strong protests. Both she and Noach blame themselves for not hiding Ben. After he is taken they spent much effort and money to find out about his whereabouts but do not get beyond the information that he is sent to Poland. Ben's deportation is the low point of their lives, especially since they think their own actions could have prevented it. I sense that Ella in camp puts aside mourning, takes time out to focus on her own survival. She cloaks herself in Noach's determination to survive. She totally enters the struggle for survival and concentrates on that. Is it her way of avenging her son? Is she standing in for him? Is her hope of seeing him again motivation for staying alive? What they do to her she cannot control, but what she can control, she does. She washes regularly and attends to her feet. And keeps an eye on me.

Ella becomes a full-time *Häftling*, prisoner. Not me. Not yet. Not fully. She does not steal; stealing from bunkmates is disdained but goes on. From the kitchen or storage rooms, workplace—yes, steal if you can. But she has no such opportunities. Barter is verboten, but acceptable and essential to the prisoners. "Organizing," the camp synonym for obtaining extra food, clothing, and better work, is an essential means of surviving. You do it for a friend or a friend does it for you. The stolen potato gets shared.

Ella has discipline—she barters, giving up bread for rags or socks. She tells me we should share one of our soups and save the other— says soup gets thicker when cold and is more filling. On the days when she is at work, I guard the soup. It is harder to guard it from myself than from others. I lick around the edges when I cannot help it. But later, when I am in Revier, in hospital, and get an extra potato, I sometimes save my bread for her. We look out for each other.

Helping Ella with some saved-up bread or just by guarding her rags and soup bowl I view as resistance—small voluntary kindnesses in this hell of brutality, where every voluntary kindness is crushed, is a touch of home and resistance. They view helping as sabotage.

## Ravensbrück friend

In no other
place can a
friend
say and do
and be
a friend
of
such magnitude
as here
where a friend
can say
and
do and be
so minimally

Once I see Ella at her most vulnerable. She stands on line for soup. After the Blockälteste ladles it into her bowl, Ella pauses for an instant, perhaps hoping for a potato from the bottom of the cauldron. The Blockälteste puts down the ladle, and then with all her might smacks Ella across the face, knocking down her soup as well. Ella picks up the empty bowl and moves on.

Neither says a word. Ella looks so humiliated, much more so than pained, though her face is red with the mark of that woman's hand. This is so personal. Such humiliation touches the core.

Ella will experience worse things—extreme hunger, hard work, excruciating thirst—but this first slap will stay with her forever, an indelible mark. The Blockälteste is less than half Ella's age. I witness the slap and do not mention it. She would prefer it that way. Hates to be pitied. I push my soup towards her, unobtrusively. This is not allowed. Verboten. She takes a few spoonfuls and says, "I am not hungry." Not hungry are not Ravensbrück words. There are humiliations that make you un-hungry.

Ella knows no one will come to her aid. We have witnessed the consequences of helping publicly—both victim and helper are tortured or killed. Prisoners are at the total mercy of anyone in authority, even other prisoners. There is no recourse. Help has to be furtive, cautious.

How did this pretty Polish Blockälteste with her faulty German become them? There are no SS around, and still she acts brutish. She stands in for them. How did they turn her against us, against herself? More bread, more soup, a coat, a clean blanket in a private room—powerful motivators, powerful corruptors. Anyone in authority, on any level, can and does to us—whatever. No accountability.

The only thing forbidden along authority lines is for SS to have sex with prisoners. Though there are rumors...

# Chapter Six

## The Apple Eater

### NEED FOR MIRACLES

December, 1944. Ravensbrück

Chanukah. Festival of miracles. Festival of light. As in those days of old, this place too is in need of a miracle. A miracle, but not lights. This dark world is too harshly lit already. Every illuminated scene hurts the eye. We need an exodus miracle—OUT OF HERE.

We need a Kurima miracle, where living things grow and expand.

Here living things are unhinged. Women shrink and shrivel. Terror shrinks us into silence. Into death.

Kurima, where water moves, water is drinkable, where water cleanses the body and quenches thirst.

Water here is dangerous. Brown, slimy, rusty, poisonous. It imparts typhoid, cramps, and death. The tap is empty, the ditch dry. They allow rainwater to drench us—they do not allow us to drink it.

Kurima with plum trees and shade trees. Crickets and dew and corn and corn-flowers and full uddered cows and clumsy calves and blacksmith tones.

Here trees make gallows, sturdy, much used gallows. Nothing green grows here. Here nature abstains. Starved women quickly, furtively, uproot the few shoots of grass between the cement cracks.

In Kurima hunger is a temporary discomfort, making for pleasant anticipation.

Not here. Hunger here is omnipresent, everlasting, eternal. Here nothing sticks. The empty soup flows quickly through. Here women's bodies have outlines, but no substance.

In Kurima horses pull plows. Here women push boulders up hill. Here women push carts with the dead or almost dead.

In Kurima fathers protect. Fathers provide.

Here childless fathers are too deplenished to mourn, too shamed by powerlessness, too dead by futile heroism. Protecting is prohibited, punishment death. Be here a father and son among the thousand, thousand—that father and son—must deny kinship. Family dismemberment is the rule. Family boundaries are of one, or less.

Mothers braid daughters' hair in Kurima.

Here, no hair.

In Kurima we built for God sanctuaries. A synagogue, a church, a chapel. Tall edifices with ornaments.

Here the watchtowers stand tall. Eternal flames illuminate the gas chamber and crematoria.

We do not want this place lighted—WE WANT OUT!

**The apple eater.** Women do not menstruate in camp. I think they put something into our soup. Some say bromide, others say it is the harsh camp conditions.

We carry all our possessions with us. The soup bowl around the waist, strung through a string and the spoon. And the small square towel, which also serves as head kerchief.

I find a postcard. A reproduction of "a young woman" by a Dutch painter. This card I keep folded in my shoe. An image to strive for? To own such a postcard is forbidden. Here things are either ordered or *verboten*. Nothing is optional.

I never see a prayer book in Ravensbrück. Punishment death. I never see a book. I never see a photograph. Never a baby bottle. I once see an apple in Ravensbrück. The SS guard walks by. She is dressed warmly and eats the apple. We all look. I think of the casualness of her. She is not even eating to provoke, just eating an apple, casually. How came she by such casualness? I know how we victims are made. How was she? We should know.

## Ravensbrück Apple-Eater

I once saw an apple
in Ravensbrück.
The apple-eater
with her black boots
a whip
and warm, warm coat —
but we the hungry
saw the apple
only.
What do You see, Lord?
Do you no longer
kick apple-eaters
out of Paradise?
— that Ravensbrück Paradise?
Explain, please.

In this paradise the apple-eaters rule. They eat the forbidden fruit and forbid us life. They are clad, and rob us of clothing. Make us naked. They eat casually and starve us planfully. Here in Ravensbrück the apple stands out because the hunger stands out. Food. It signifies food.

We want God to intervene, hand *us* the apple.

**Strickerinnen.** The special group of women in our block sits together and knits. *Strickerinnen*, knitters, firmly established in the main hall, knit socks and gloves for German soldiers at the Russian front. They are envied because the work is light. They stay indoors and get extra soup. They are never punished. They are secure in their importance, providing warmth for soldiers of the Fatherland.

The wool is brown and dark green. Monotonous. Are they thinking of the bright colors of before? All you see is deep concentration as the thin needles shift around in circles, making green gloves, brown socks. Such knitting requires much skill and experience. The women give it all.

An announcement is made, "Strickerinnen, gather in the main hall." Soon they are helped onto trucks. They are being "relocated to a less crowded" place. Perhaps by some miracle that may even be so. We connect survival with miracles and SS "relocation" with death. We are onto their euphemisms, so what? The Strickerinnen look so betrayed. So numbed by shock.

We hear of Strickerinnen engaging in sabotage, knitting four fingered gloves or socks without openings. But these women here look very dutiful, very law abiding. I hope that if any one of them did engage in sabotage, she will have a brief smile of satisfaction on the way to... not much to smile about. Not a time for smiling.

Replacements come all the time. Soon a new group of women take up the knitting project. They think they are so fortunate to land this easy work. And who knows... perhaps a miracle...

Some Strickerinnen may be grandmothers, it is hard to tell age here. Grandmothers are not wanted here. A world of women and no grandmothers?

Will "grandmother" be just an archaic word?

**Mail.** Jews are not allowed mail or packages. Some others are... German political prisoners, Poles, French resistance workers. The incoming and outgoing mail is naturally censored; different categories of prisoners have different rules regarding size and frequency. Some women even receive packages from the Red Cross.

"Superior—Inferior" must be mapped onto their soul. Even in this place they create such ranks, such categories.

To whom would Jews write? Who would be there to receive the mail, write back?

Is there one intact Jewish family in all of Czechoslovakia, Holland, Hungary, Poland, Lithuania, Greece? Is there one Jewish family who lives in a house with food and wrapping paper and a post office nearby? One who knows where their missing son or mother is? Senders have nothing to send and nowhere to send it to. Senders do not exist and we cannot receive. *Verboten.*

I would like a meal with no sand and no ROT. Manna would do. I would make it taste like poppy seed cake and buttermilk...for taste and smell of home.

> I will send this letter from my brain
> and you will get it right away
> Come and get me
> *Come and get me*
> I am ready...

Somebody, somebody, come and get me. Roosevelt, where are you? You tarry like our Messiah. Note, we do not have messianic

eons here. No messianic time frame. Time ends at the whim of an
SS, of starvation, in the quarry, of typhus, next day, next minute.

## Come Messiah

Come, Messiah
when blossoms quiver
the cow is milked
children bathed
and done with measles
the week's Torah
portion read
and fathers rest.

If this is not
convenient, ordained
or appropriate
come then in times
of empty udders,
typhoid, lice and lamentations,
prayers said — not read
(the Written Word
in flames of amber was
returned to the Sender)
It would suit us fine
if you made this
Messiah time

Is not the Apocalypse
your cue
to do
the Messiah thing?

Ravensbrück Concentration Camp
Germany
Winter, 1944

President Franklin D. Roosevelt
The White House
America

Dear President Roosevelt,

I can only identify myself by my number. Prisoners here are not allowed to use their names. My number is #83,621. That indicates that 83,620 women came here before me. Since my arrival here last year the numbers are much higher. New prisoners arrive every day in large numbers, many from Auschwitz, which is being evacuated due to the Russian advances.

I cannot give you my name, but, Mr. President, I know your name. Your name was a household word in our household in Czechoslovakia. Your name was always said with reverence and respect. No jokes were told about you. A serious man for serious times. A good man for bad times. Hitler hates, but Roosevelt cares. He took care of the poor in America; he will take care of the persecuted in Europe. As certain it is that Tuesday follows Monday, so certain are we that you will win the war—with the help of Churchill and Stalin.

Timing. Most of those with convictions of your victory are no longer here for vindication. To die here of natural causes takes two to three months. Of unnatural causes, days, seconds, eternities. Leather shoes and a potato prolong life if you are not subject to whims, whips, dog bites, typhoid. There is no safe corner here. The margin between life and death is microscopic.

My Aunt Ella, who is here with me, says, "Mrs. Roosevelt has sensible shoes. I would give five bread rations for those shoes." I say to her, " If you gave up five bread rations, you would not need those shoes."

Mr. Roosevelt, President, we need to get out of here. Open the gates. Do not be fooled by the "*Arbeit Macht Frei*" sign over the gate, as we were. Their intended and carried-out goal is "*Vernichtung durch Arbeit*"—Himmler's orders—annihilate them through work. My request, my urgent request—Go by our time. Not by outside time. Greetings. Shalom.

#83,621

P.S. Jewish prisoners are not allowed mail. We cannot send it nor receive it. So here then is my own name—Judita Sternova of Czechoslovakia.

Thousands, millions, such letters are written to you from Sachsenhausen, Buchenwald, Auschwitz, Dachau, Theresienstadt. I vouch for their accuracy, urgency. Though not sent—read them. Go by our time, President Roosevelt.

**Appell.** Roll call. The wake up siren sounds at four a.m.—the sound of dread and ugliness. To help me get up I have developed a system that works for me—"resistance" I call it and get up. Family injunction in operation. The other option to getting up is being beaten to death, thrown into the punishment bunker, bullets—but "resistance" works for me—a gift to the family, a gift from the family. And Ella's example . . . she rises unhesitatingly, to avoid the daily whips and screams of *Aufstehen*—get up!

Not everyone rises. Many die during the night and some risk tortured death rather than face another day. It is not the early hour of rising; it is all the hours of wakefulness.

> it is the day ahead
> that shrieks
> no more, no more,
> no more, of that

At four a.m. I rush to the lavatories before the long line forms. Appell is at five a.m., but to stand a long time on line and cope with diarrhea, dysentery—not enough lavatories—not enough time. Never toilet paper. I also rush to the washroom. The dead women from the night before have not been brought in yet. The floor is less crowded. Coffee also motivates me. Dark grey water it is, but hot. We make beds according to regulations...louse-infested, pus-stained blankets, but sharp, neat, corners.

My waking hours are spent on survival efforts. My nighttime hours, my nightmares, are usually of being pursued. I am trying to protect someone—a child. We are on the run. Is it Mirjam? She is in hiding. I worry about her. Miss her. Some variations, but the child and pursuit dream theme is constant. Once I dream plates of food are placed in front of me, I can choose, but every portion contains poison.

On a good night my dream is of food. I dream I am eating.

Punishment for being late for Appell, severe beating, kneeling outside on concrete pebbles all day without food or water, or any other punishment the guard orders. For the infraction of one prisoner, a guard can also impose punishment on the whole block. They rush us *schnell* to Appell to keep us standing still.

The overnight dead, every night people die, left in their bunks till after Appell are included in the count. Present, in whatever way—alive or dead—the numbers must add up.

A daily accounting of about 120,000 prisoners. The numbers change daily.

Transports leave, new prisoners arrive, newly dead, selections— SS concern is the accurate count. Not how, just how many.

We stand outside on the Appell Platz, square. Thousands and thousands, hours and hours. They count the standing, they count the lying in hospital, they count the newly dead, the collapsed. There are some exceptions to standing Appell, but no one is exempt from the count. The missing will be found and we stand silent and wait for the find. No help is allowed for anyone who collapses.

## During Appell

When she fell
during appel
the women around her
being new
bent down towards her
— automatic responses still —
they never straightened up
could not
after shots and dogs
— this did nor affect
the body count

Appell. Today a woman runs suddenly from the Appell line— she runs towards the electrified fence. The dog gets to her before she reaches it. Screaming, she tries to push the dog away. She kicks and her shoe falls off; she must have treasured those shoes, leather shoes, not wooden clogs. The animal is not called back, he attacks until there is no more movement. Every horrified one of us wants to rush out and help—no one does. Silence. There are so many of us here, how are we so crushed into silence and inaction? The reason right there, in front of us—they watch us closely, provocatively, hand on the trigger and dogs at the ready— hoping for another futile sacrifice. They render us debilitatingly powerless. Life directed moves get cut down. At rare times we can help, furtively, secretly. This occasion allows us nothing. Help is sabotage, going against the order. We are filled with rage and pity and helplessness and are paralyzed by their brutality. Certainty is with them; they never hesitate. And guns too. How purposeful they look, how useless we.

Felicie Mertens, "Appellstehen—Roll Call." Courtesy of
Sammlungen Ravensbrück.

The SS woman now stands in front of our Appell group and
talks about the danger of breaking the law.

What is she saying? That we risk death by choosing death? You
stupid SS! Can we choose life by abiding by the law? Your law—
our life preserver? Is it not your law that brings us here to die? Stop
that crazy talk! Stop! Stop!

The body of the dead woman is hoisted onto a pole, and for
additional two Appell hours we are forced to stand and watch her
shoeless, brutalized, hanging body.

I do not know the Kaddish, the memorial prayer, so I say
the Shema, without moving my lips... prayer is forbidden. Hear,
O' Israel... I do not expect Him to hear. I say it for her benefit and
mine. Another breech of Ravensbrück law. Another futile gesture.

Standing in the back is preferable. Less visibility is always safer.
Attention never draws a positive response. Here for extinction,

existence is resistance. A live Jew—a failure on their part? An unfinished job? Jews get the hardest job assignments under the worst camp conditions. *Vernichtung durch Arbeit.* Other prisoners are worked, starved, abused, but as a group Jews are singled out for the worst. Gypsies too. Gypsies are not abused as badly, but they are systematically killed in large numbers.

If the Appell numbers tally, we are released after two to three hours. If not, the guards get meaner, the dogs more restless, prison officials more nervous, while we the standing shift from shivers and boredom to anxiety and terror. No talking or stretching is allowed. In winter diarrhea stains are seen on the snow; this too is verboten. Another reason no one wants to stand in the front row.

The night ends with Appell, the day starts with Appell. The day no one wants is here. All pray to live another day. We pray to a God we have given up on—we still believe in divine miracles.

Appell. A prisoner in the third row shifts her arm and a raw potato falls out from her sleeve. The potato rolls forward and before she can retrieve it an SS is upon her. She pulls the woman out of line and orders the five prisoners in the front row to beat and kick her. Those who resist are lash whipped by the other guards present. Guards stand around in hooded capes and boots and laugh.

They are not cold. Not thin, not hungry. Not scared. Nor frostbitten. Not dog bitten. Not whip beaten. Their coats get warmer as the weather gets colder. Their dogs, too, get coats. They expand as we shrink. So secure, so un-hesitant. Do they learn in victim-making schools this *Übermensch*, this *Untermensch* stuff? Superior/inferior—their obsession! They would rather be here than anywhere else in the Reich.

After Appell the beaten woman is carried off by prisoners. She is thrown onto a pile of dead bodies.

God, one potato, one raw potato—the woman stole one raw potato to stay alive one more day. A raw potato. It is not possible to tell her age, she could be twenty or fifty, with the weight of a child. She is beaten to death for us to see. Punishment is usually public, attendance and observation for such crimes, compulsory. When it is not public, then we imagine the torture in the punishment block, in the bunker, the hanging, the shooting behind the wall.

## Let not flowers here

Let not flowers here
   not scented rose
   not meadow hues
   not daffodils
   not gentle dew

a bird in flight
would fry
in voltaged walls
higher than the sky

no Edenic scenes for me
Edenic scenes a mockery,
crushed and crazed
indignant

I would be
when tortured
amidst
splendidry

Appell. January. I stand in the freezing rain. When Appell is finally over I feel a strange discomfort—confused I say to Ella, "Why is my dress so stiff around me?" She checks me and says, "Your dress froze on you."

    They worry about escape? There are very few. How escape, in wooden clogs, swollen sores, electric fences, bodies emptied of

Helen Ernst, "Ohne Titel—Untitled." Courtesy of Museum Schwerin.

energy? Work outside the camp is supervised by Kapos, prisoner wardens, and dogs. Only the privileged look fit enough, they are the least likely to attempt a run. They worry about escapees?

Would you escape knowing of the reprisals? Of hostage shootings—every fifth or eighth or tenth woman in line?

There are more suicides than escapes. Suicide too is an ordeal. A prisoner running to the electric fence is likely to be shot by the watchtower guard or mauled by a dog. Orders. They are in charge of death. They forbid death by suicide. Suicide is not on their approved death list. *Musulman* deaths are allowed. No one stops Musulman from dying. Musulman women seem indifferent to what goes on around them. Women who disconnect. They no longer kill lice. They no longer guard their shoes. Make no moves to avoid the wind. They let go of all the needs of life. Survival here requires such commitment of will and luck. Letting go even a little leads to Musulman status. Not washing. Not eating the slimy soup with rotten turnips. Musulman women are numb outside and numb inside. Numb inside? Numb inside? Who knows what life, what memory, what love, peace or rage, what passion is within her?

Women shuffle into death for so many reasons. Or perhaps just one—this Ravensbrück life. Un-life.

I dare not look too closely at Musulman women, for fear it is catching. How do I not look? Where is it safe to look? Death, where are you not?

God. Did your angels draw your attention to these women? The women who bathed children. Slept in beds. Lit Shabbat candles. Practiced medicine. Bought hats. Studied music. Grew sweet peas and anemones. Laughed.

Fire those angels who fail to make you take note. Those of old were more alert . . . Isaac was saved, but who today is staying the hand of children's slayers? Mourning mothers are among the Musulman women.

**The body.** When a new, pretty woman comes into our block, I make an assessment—two, three weeks before she no longer recognizes herself? The absence of mirrors will spare her the shock.

Does she remember still the taste of peppermint toothpaste? The feel of a toothbrush?

Does she know she arrived into a shrinking world? She will—she may—have days, but not everyday things.

I hate this. I hate it.

My fourteen-year-old body is a liability. I feel its burden through the lice in my hair, the bloodied scratches on back and arms. Through the cold that invades my every cell. The hurt of hunger and agony of thirst. The harsh, steady cough deprives me of vanished energy. Sleep is of nightmares. In spite of our scarecrow thinness, our narrow bunk is still too narrow for the four of us—the bloodstained blanket too thin and the non-existent mattress too non-existent.

We are not allowed shade from sun or shelter from rain.

My body itches, craves, pesters. Wants, wants. Gives no rest, provides no pleasure—just occasional reprieve. My body is the center. My body is a liability. And I, and I try, with all my might (might?) to hold on to it. Once you let the body go—give in to lice, cold, hurt, it goes—the direction is always death.

**Sick.** It is winter. It is snowing. Out there you can say it like that—it is winter, it is snowing.

## Snow.

Snow, I remember you —
you settled on my orange
cap and matching boots
(new, for I was expecting you)
then hand in hand
we traversed my universe
from Poplar Bend to

Post Office to Marta's place —
to let her see
my finery

Look all. Calm, slow
in steady flow
snow transformed into one hue
this brightly messy
neighborhood
Monochromatic artistry!
the girl in orangery
laughs at this audacity

Not here, snow. Our rusted leaking roofs, gaping window frames, shuffling feet cannot cope with snow. Go where poplars grow.

When you are cold in Ravensbrück, you do not get warmer, just less cold, if you are lucky. When you are hungry, just less hungry, if you are lucky. Options for the better are minimal, unpredictable, forbidden, stymied. They say this is the coldest winter in Europe. It is. Record snow falls.

I am sick. I cough and my cough does not get better. Being sick is bad news. My cough does not improve. Not after all those hours of Appell in rain and cold, diarrhea from the soup, weakness from—the whole mess.... Seeking help is very risky. The Blockälteste insists I go to the clinic. I go in fear. The clinic is still clean at this time. Medical personnel wear white coats. No doubt for the benefit of Red Cross inspectors. (The Red Cross inspectors are shown whatever the SS want them to see. Certain sections are prettied up and activities staged for the benefit of the Red Cross. This farcical deception works, inspections pass.)

I'm examined in the clinic and X-rayed. Then without any explanation a procedure called pneumothorax is performed. Air is pumped into my lungs, or around my lungs. Apart from the needle insert, this is not particularly uncomfortable. My fear and ignorance are overwhelming. The treatment is performed by a Czech prison doctor, with an SS physician present. I am told to report to Block 10 and come back for treatment at a given time.

Medical experiments are being carried out in Ravensbrück. The subjects are women prisoners. This information is highly secret, but it is whispered about. Those whispers are now screams in my ears.

*"Du wirst ja besser warden."* You are sure to get better, says the Blockälteste. She does not sound convincing and marks my departure in her Appell record book. I say goodbye to Ella and bunkmates, and we promise to keep in touch.

Ella says, "Try not to stay there long. Come back even if you are not fully recovered." I know she is thinking of the three women from our Block who went to the hospital and did not come back. I am thinking the same, in addition to the medical experiments, which are more terrifying to me. When Ella is worried she sounds tough, like now. With spoon and bowl I leave. Now I am all alone. Until now I was always in the company of someone I knew. In Ravensbrück, it is essential to know someone. To keep an eye on your bowl, on you. To push a little when you think you cannot face another Appel or work assignment. Someone you can count on. Will share a stolen potato or a bartered bread ration. Someone who wants you to live. Someone who knows you are a friend even if you are not allowed to show it.

To date Ella and I have been a family and we adopt Hanicka, who comes on the same transport with us. But Hanicka is soon chosen for work in a sub-camp. Her chosen group consists of young, healthy newcomers; we are hopeful that she is indeed chosen for work and not "selected" for...

My new Hungarian friend is Magda. Though Ella is our "mother" figure, she is not sentimental, she models toughness, survival commitment, so I sometimes hold Magda in my arms and stroke her hairless head. Magda dies in her bunk. Family membership can be very short-lived.

Related and camp families try hard to stay together. Always that fear—separation means finality. Ella and I take "being there for each other" for granted. Newly formed families count on each other as well. Women not connected to others drift easily into "Musulman" status.

I tell no one about that pneumothorax, then or after.

I feel incredible shame of being a subject of experiments, an involuntary subject to what end? Of my personal death I still cannot conceive—but this is horror. I feel totally controlled by evil. An involuntary subject. This is how it is with animals, they have no say. My life they declare worthless, my medical condition is of value to German medical "science." Will they inject me with an illness or treat mine with some untried experimental method?

My main awareness is shame. I am possessed by shame. I will tell no one; no one is to see me through my eyes. Pity would shame me further.

Camp experiments are of bone transplants. The goal is to obtain replacement parts for wounded German soldiers. New medicines are also sought for the treatment of infections. Prisoners are injected with substances, which produce gangrene, or with the gangrene itself and are then treated with these new experimental drugs. Very few survive.

I do not know if that pneumothorax is within the experimental category. I do later recover, my lungs are healthy, but that shame remains. That shame is theirs—say I—hand it over. But it sticks.

**Revier.** Hospital. Block 10 is the TB block. Block 11 the typhoid block. Both well known in the camp. Both to be avoided. Patients do not receive treatment in either block, but they are spared Appell and work assignments. A few get better, most do not. Even if they could, they are not given time enough for recovery. Those suffering from typhus—spread by the lice—are totally isolated

Maria Hiszpanska, "Läuse suchen—Looking for Lice." Courtesy of Sammlungen Ravensbrück.

in their blocks. There to die. The block has one advantage; fearing contagion, the SS stay away. Here typhoid is the only thing they are cautious about, at all else they go full force.

The other main advantage of all Reviers—no Appell and no work—could be a life-saver, if not for the frequent selections. Life-killers.

Revier—another euphemism—is a way stations rather than hospital. Hardly any medication is given. Patients are not even allowed a bed long enough to die in—if they do not recover quickly or die quickly, they are "relocated." In Revier you need someone to pay special attention to you, take risks on your behalf, preferably someone in authority.

In my TB block white-coated personnel come by daily and take everyone's temperature. Periodically those with temperature above a certain degree are "removed." Survival is measured by miracles. A miracle that saves you from death today is as far as your future is assured in Revier.

In my entire life my body temperature registers below normal, including while in Block 10.

Miraculously, Block 10 proves life enhancing for me—for the moment. Erika Buchmann is the Blockälteste. She is a German political prisoner, brought here in 1939 after serving in several other prisons. She was released and imprisoned again. Erika pays lifesaving attention to me. Says I remind her of her daughter Inge, whom she has not seen since her imprisonment. But I learn she helps all those she can. She puts an extra potato into my soup, smiles when I go by, and takes me to the clothing storage where I'm given a warm sweater. When I put it on, a large X is painted all across the back in thick, white paint, which is totally indelible, not a speck ever comes off. A warm sweater warms you and your outlook. The sweater is great but soon becomes lice-infested—even more so than my red cotton dress. I am embarrassed to search for lice in the company of others. Soon the three of us who share the bottom bunk make this into a social activity. I become expert at finding and crushing lice, but they are always ahead of me in numbers, itching, biting. Is it my own blood I am crushing out of them?

The large hall is filled with three tiered bunks. Three of us to each one. My initial bunkmates are Sofia from Vienna and Milka from Yugoslavia. Sofia is beautiful, beautiful in the manner of a porcelain doll, pale and dainty. She is fifteen. She talks exclusively about how her mother, Mutti, is sure to find her. That is all. Not about going home, only about being with mother, wherever. I have similar thoughts, but my reunion is not for here and I do not talk about it.

but you know what I wish, that I would not have to miss?
that place in the shade of the trees with the plums
where you could rest — and make dreams
and when you were glad and when you were sad
after a while you would wait for the smile
for after a while — your mother would bring
*a smile and a drink.*
Nice, those feasts under the trees!

Because we are young we also have young memories.

I say jokingly, "When I looked in the mirror at home, I worried about freckles, big ears, and my very, very, extremely, very straight hair. What about you?"

Milka stops searching for lice and jumps up, hitting her head on the bunk above. She laughs. "It is the opposite with me, exactly the opposite! My hair is so curly that I used to sleep with a wet kerchief to straighten it. Didn't work!"

Her head is shaved, and we take her word regarding the curls.

Now Milka and I look at Sophia. She smiles, slowly. And takes her time, as though she wants to hold on to the smile.

"Mutti always said in all of Vienna no one has a daughter more beautiful than I. It is because your papa is not Jewish." Sophia often talks about her mother, but I have never seen her smile before. She is beautiful.

Shock and anger, my immediate reaction to her remark. I could tell her about my beautiful cousins and friends who have Jewish mothers AND Jewish fathers. But I say nothing. Let her have her smile.

Milka is not Jewish. Sophia's remark does not slap her. These words just noises to her. Milka is tough. (How tough if she lands in the TB wards?) She talks about her experiences as a partisan.

She is no more than sixteen. She was caught carrying messages between partisan groups.

Such pride: "I never got lost in the forests. My partisans could always count on me. They knew I would find them, even if they had to move around." She gives detailed descriptions of how she memorized the secret messages. Was she tortured into divulging these messages? I do not ask.

Milka is befriended by a Czech doctor who arranges for her transfer. For now she is saved. Sofia is selected. We do not call it that, just "gone." Gone also her replacements. Gone where? No one is informed. We all know and hope we do not. Gas chambers are operating. When someone is removed, I block out imagining the next step. I try to block it out.

You see the sores of frozen feet, dog bites, and bruises. The sores are visible—there are no bandages.

Marina in the bunk above is a Russian prisoner of war. She comes from a part of Russia that was previously Poland. Polish and Slovak are similar enough for us to understand each other, enough. Her hair has grown back so she must be here long enough to have contracted whatever brings her to Revier. She says she is a parachutist and that pride of accomplishment shines in her. She wears the striped prison camp dress and ties it around her waist with a men's necktie. The tie is faded and frayed. Did she bring it with her? Did she barter for it? Who owned it? If an item is not of the standard striped camp uniform, it has a story. I have seen here the most bizarrely inappropriate clothing issued to women—evening gowns and ballet skirts and high heeled shoes—but Marina's necktie is somehow unique. It brings echoes of respect and dignity of another world, a purposeful luxury. Marina wears it around her waist, but ties it into a necktie knot. Because she treats this tie so personally I do not ask about it. We stay away from the personal.

Marina tells me, "I am a soldier of the Soviet Union, a parachutist. I should be in a prisoner-of-war-camp, not in a concentration camp. But you know the Germans!"

I say to Marina, "Write a letter of complaint to the Commandant of the camp. Tell him that your friend, Judita, has complaints as well."

Marina looks at me stunned, then bursts out laughing—a big strong laugh.

"A letter to the Commandant" becomes our private code... and our complaint list is long.

Marina urges me to get out of Revier as soon as I can. "This is not a safe place. You must leave!" Over and over... "you must out." One day she wraps her frozen feet (she has several toes missing) into pieces of the blanket she tears up. If she is reported they will kill her for this act of "sabotage." Damaging Reich property is forbidden, seen as a subversive act. Shuffling, Marina leaves the barrack. She returns the same day. She could not even walk to the fence and sat hidden somewhere outside our block. After this episode she is much more subdued—as though she tested the limits of survival and failed.

Those who do not recuperate quickly are "removed." "Quickly" may just be the time between selections, sometimes days—sometimes weeks. Marina does not look at me when they carry her out. Marina is twenty-three. She wants to be twenty-four and twenty-five and forty-seven...

Tears come, which surprises me. I thought my tears were dried into numbness already.

### Reluctant Witness

Am I to be that mariner
And re-tell that tale of yesteryear?
I am not him
I did not sin
Call upon them
Who dismembered the Sun!

   ...

I testify
To their murder of:

Anna — death by starving
Evka — death by beating
Daniel — death by gassing
Lily's son — by hanging
Ivan — typhoid
Stephano — drowning
Johanna — starving and shooting
Mrs. Rheinhardt — by choice — to avoid the above
Chayim — death by living

Where is the judge?
Where are you, judge?
Is there a judge?

In Revier, we do not stand Appell. Many here are unable to do so anyway, but in the other blocks, physical disability is not an excuse, just a reason for shooting or gassing. No Appell in Revier. But I have an image from there that I cannot erase or weaken. It is in my eyes, my ears, in my skin. Off the corridor leading to the washroom is a room. It is small and crowded with *die Verückten*, the crazies. There are no bunks in there, not enough blankets. Kept in there until taken out to be killed, with no possibility to leave that room. When they are taken out, some are naked. I hear them scream, shout, fight, cry.

I do not know what constitutes madness in Ravensbrück— crying too much for a lost child? Getting into a squabble? Displeasing a person in authority—even a prisoner in authority? Losing one's mind, attempting suicide at the electric fence? Ravensbrück is madness, but these women whom THEY label mad are locked up and soon taken away. The empty room is quickly filled again. I hear the screaming ones and the silent ones.

### The Invitation

Would You come down

that ladder — that ladder
Jacob climbed?
I will not deal with angels
I'll wait till You arrive.
When You come down
that ladder — that ladder
Jacob climbed
then I will take Your hand
and I will be Your
guide and
I will showYou sights
not fit
for Godly eyes
(not fit for thee
is it for me?)
who will make it fit for Thee?

For Your divine grief
I would hand a handkerchief,
I have none
nor am I in need of one,
we drink our tears
— water shortage

If Erika puts an extra potato into my soup, or I get an occasional
slice of cheese, I save my bread for Aunt Ella. Ella is working outdoors now. She is even more hungry

This day too I meet Ella at the fence separating the Revier
from the rest of the camp. This inside fence is not electrified;
we can touch hands. As I pass over the bread, *"Du blöde Schwein,
das ist verboten! Verboten. Halt!"* You stupid swine, this is forbidden! The SS from Ella's side of the fence rushes over, grabs
the bread out of Ella's hand, beats her with the rifle butt, shoves
the bread under her nose, and flings it away. Several women rush

Maria Hiszpanska, "Szenen aus dem Lagerleben—Scenes of camp life." Courtesy of Sammlungen Ravensbrück.

for it. Lashing out with the rifle, he is after them. They take the beating and the bread. A bread ration is about four inches wide.

To improve your life beyond the minimum conditions they allow is forbidden. Forbidden also is to help others. I watch a sister trying to take her younger sibling's place on a work line because the sibling is not well—she is weak from dysentery— an SS guard notices and beats her to death. They use violence with such ease. No hesitation. Beating to death, the whip or rifle butt on the woman's body, opening the skin, crushing the bones. I have never seen a reluctant beating. They may look indifferent, bored even, but never reluctant. I force myself to watch, to give her a human connection, even if she remains unaware or unconscious. How do you unlearn to protect a sister? In this Ravensbrück re-education camp, you not only learn new, crazy, unheard-of things, they want you also to unlearn long-taught, ingrained things. Kindness is sabotage. Please God, do not let me get used to everything.

You stupid, stupid SS guard! Do you think Ella will be less hungry tomorrow? With my next potato, I am saving my bread for her. But we will both be more cautious.

**Regina.** Regina from the bottom bunk of my previous block comes to the fence. She arrives in Ravensbrück with another woman. They both come with babies and occupy the adjoining lower bunks. I watch how hard each tries to keep her baby alive. Now Regina at the fence says, "My baby died." Regina looks empty and worn. She does not cry. I do not cry. I do not cry much in Ravensbrück. Though this is a time for crying. For raging. For smashing up the world. For ripping bark off trees. For puncturing God's eardrums.

I do not ask her, did you place the baby on the cold washroom floor? How long before they took her? Did you have something to wrap her in? Did you watch? These questions should not be asked. Should not be answered. Should not be. But I have them. Some questions do not leave you . . . answered or unanswered.

I do not console Regina. How? We stand silent on either side of the fence. I do not offer her the half potato I have saved. Today her baby died of starvation; today Regina will not eat just to stay alive. Today she does not feel her own hunger. Today Regina needs time to mourn. Today she eats pain. She does not want to return to the block where her baby lies naked on the cold washroom floor, but Ravensbrück does not provide a place where mothers can sit shiva. Not a place, not a time, for mourning. Only the cause.

Mourning here must be short-lived. Mourning ceases or the mourner dies. All will and energy is needed to make it from Appell to Appell.

I know later, back in the block, Aunt Ella will tell Regina she must stay alive for her son, Sam. Sam is eleven. He is in the men's section with his father. Regina has not heard from either since her arrival. Regina will not hear Ella who will nevertheless prod her along, march next to her numbed body to work, and perhaps succeed.

I ask Regina to come back to the fence tomorrow—I am not allowed into the main camp yet. I will give her my saved half potato then. I must not—must not eat it.

We cannot take away her grief, just help her postpone it. Help her hang on. Alone she will not make it.

This is a place of pain and terror for everyone, but especially for parents—because they cannot protect their children. Women have the extremes of pain because all younger children go with their mothers and mothers are unable to mother.

Regina, if you survive, where will you put your grief? Will you have more babies? Will you name one Naomi—after little Naomi on the shower-room floor? Will you try to erase this image? How? What a task survival will be.

The other baby in the Block dies also.

### Ravensbrück Mother

The baby died
not all at once.
The mother took it
back into her womb
the baby was willing, but

soon the juices stopped flowing.
I walked by
and saved my screams
for later

Lord that particular
pain is too much
for me
You have it
and be
branded

**Such experts.** They are such experts at humiliation. They negate even their smallest gesture of humanity. Erika from the hospital takes me to the clothing depot where I am given that sweater—brown, thick, hand-knitted. Like all non-prison uniforms, the large white X painted across the back is larger than life, more permanent than any life here. I am here long enough not to wonder who owned this sweater before me. I revel in its warmth. It stays on my back, over the red polka-dot dress, all through my imprisonment.

On the way back to the Revier, Erika is stopped by an SS guard. It is a friendly meeting. They obviously know each other. Erika is an old-timer, a German political prisoner of some importance. I am astounded by their camaraderie; they chat like equals. And suddenly the guard whips Erika across her arm and then again across her shoulder. Full force. Erika's lips quaver. She looks surprised, says nothing. I know the lash is not the result of their talk, just small talk.

Is that the SS woman's way of re-establishing their roles? A prisoner and guard are not equal, is she reminding them both? The whip reclaims the essence of the place—power, superiority, violence. I am more surprised by the friendly interaction than by the whip. Erika's facial expression says, "Did you have to?" A prisoner of many years she needs no reminding. I hate being witness to such scenes. Humiliations bruise the core.

They cannot let it be. Human gestures are negated. This harshened woman crushes the bones of the one who cares for the sick, then walks away with ease. What is she thinking? Is she thinking?

Does she shift into *Menschlichkeit*, humanness, when she crosses the camp gate? She sleeps in a house, has a toothbrush, has leftover bread from breakfast, whips Erika.

**Moral musings in Ravensbrück.** Erika gives me crackers. Of course, I gladly accept these. Accept unhesitatingly and wonder involuntarily—inwardly—is she in cahoots with that SS guard? How came she by these crackers? Crackers are not on Ravensbrück prisoner menu. I would eat whatever she gave me. Gladly. But my admiration and high respect for her is shaken. Questioning the morality of oppressed victims? Such questioning is surely immoral.

When I find out that German prisoners are allowed packages from the outside, I am relieved about Erika's morality. I owe her an apology. I make it inwardly but to her I do not admit my moralizing hypocrisy. Still, I also give thanks that my moral musings are not yet beyond my capacity. Give me a little longer in here...

Winter 1945. The camp is overcrowded by new arrivals, mainly from Auschwitz and Hungary. Women from other camps arrive in terrible physical condition. Revier is more crowed, selections more frequent and even less selective. During selections I try not to cough and almost suffocate holding it in—breathing a literal sigh of life when selection officials pass.

My cough finally improves. Erika sends me out of Block 10—
"You must go out. It is not safe here." Eventually I rejoin Ella in
a sub-camp where prisoners work in the Siemens factory, manufacturing armaments for the German war industry.

# *Chapter Seven*

## Siemens Sub-Camp

**C**lose call. Ella is working in the Siemens factory, manufacturing parts for armaments. Conditions in this sub-camp are better, perhaps because Siemens prisoners work in close contact with German civilians. But the slightest infraction in the factory is seen as sabotage resulting in severe punishment, death, and quick replacement.

Appell here is shorter, the soup is thicker. However, the toilets are outside. I go there during my first night and from the watchtower the guard shouts, "Halt! Halt!" I run—he shoots. I keep running and he keeps shooting. I cannot see the bullets but hear and smell them all around me. When I manage to get back into the barrack everyone is awake, awakened by the noise outside.

The Blockälteste, dressed in a housecoat, grabs me as I enter, and yells, "Are you mad to go out there?! How can they keep a watch on you in the dark, you stupid Jew?" She does not put on the light and orders everyone back into their bunks, *schnell*! Me she drags to my bunk, pushes me up onto the second tier, and quickly covers me with the blanket I share with my bunkmates.

*"Macht alles normal! Alles normal!"* she keeps whispering anxiously and angrily up and down along the row of bunks. Order, she wants, order.

She is terrified and furious. If they come in to investigate the shooting, my behavior will be seen as an attempt to escape. Nothing enrages them more than escapes. The Blockälteste will be held responsible for my behavior, and she and the whole block will be punished. Punishment . . . they have a prescribed repertoire.

As for me . . . attempted escapees are publicly hanged or shot after torture in the punishment bunker. Age is no protection.

Since I am on the bunk above Ella's, she is not aware of my absence until my return when I am being "tucked" in by the Blockälteste.

Soon Ella whispers, "Tomorrow I will show you where the urine bucket is." That will be good. In the dark we stay indoors without lavatories. It is winter. It gets dark early. When I wake up during that night, I see Ella standing and watching me, shaking her head, covering me.

I should be worrying about hanging and shooting and torture and the pain caused others, and all I can think of is how does the Blockälteste manage to have a housecoat? She is the first and only woman I see in Ravensbrück wearing a housecoat. My thoughts will not move beyond this topic. I have been wrapped in a housecoat before. I know of that. A noose around my neck, a bullet into my body . . . my mind refuses . . .

The night passes without anyone investigating. The Blockälteste says nothing more to me, and sometimes she gives me soup from the bottom.

I work out this scenario: she owes her life to my fast running and is grateful. When I am not totally on the edge I indulge in heroic fantasies . . . at least survival fantasies.

**Jano.** Now, when I am not quite so cold, not quite so hungry, and even in Ravensbrück spring is beginning, I think of Jano. Jano from back home.

## My Ravensbrück Love Song

One Sunday
that Spring
the Sun came by.
I untangled my hair,
with the hem of my dress
wiped the mud off my shoes
then — in proper attire
I set forth

Not today
you stupid walls of ugliness!
today
I decree
plum trees, crickets and green things for
me

On the street with a name
— no numbers today —
we meet — Jano and me,
I am early
as is he
his mother liked me
"that blue-eyed girl"
would she be pleased
her Jano and me?

Stand back you stupid walls
stand back!

Today we will not be
walled in —
not Jano
not me

Of Jano I have only my fourteen-year-old fantasy. Jano dies in Auschwitz...as does his family.

I miss Erika Buchmann. I miss her tallness. In this restricted camp environment she manages to take up space, manages her visibility, and manages to remain human. She helps some, including me, and is powerless to help most. But unlike many prisoners with power, her words do not assault, her hands do not slap. Perhaps her longevity here, four years, gain her enough validation from the SS so that she does not have to prove loyalty by outperforming their brutality. Or perhaps the TB Revier, by nature of its sick population, provides enough prisoners for "selection" to satisfy them. Since she is a political prisoner she has a group of longstanding friends, a strong support system. But four years! She uses these connections to benefit others. Four years! I am inclined to be a worshipper. "Before" my mother was on the pedestal; now I put Erika there as well. Her aid and my adulation help. Survivor bricks.

In my imaginary report to Anyu, I say, "You would like Erika, she likes your daughter."

When I go to the main camp, I try to visit Erika.

**Judit.** I need permission to go into the main camp. This has to be given be the SS *Ausführerin* (overseer). She has an office within the sub-camp. Another prisoner and I go there together. The

Ausführerin sits at a large desk, crisply uniformed. The whip on the desk, the German shepherd on the floor next to her. She is young, perhaps twenty. Quite pretty. The hair under her cap is light and straight. Most of the SS women have hair permanents. I observe her unobtrusively and think she could be my older sister—we look somewhat alike. As we prisoners are entering the office she is petting the dog. I notice some mud on her boots. She asks the other prisoner her name and purpose of visit. The name given is Polish. The Ausführerin signs the permission slip and the prisoner leaves.

"*Wie heisst du?*" she asks me. What is your name?

"Judit," I say, and before I have time to give her my surname, she jumps up, grabs the whip and shouts, addressing the dog.

"What do you expect with a name like that?! Judit! Bragging about her Jewishness! The swine, does she think her damned star is a medal?! We will teach them about Jewish pride! Why does she think she is here, in this Lager? *Vernichtung!*"

The dog is now standing and pulling the leash in my direction. I do not pull away. Strangely I do not feel fear. I feel calm. For the first time in this Ravensbrück I look at an SS directly and not down as required at pain of death. She rages and I keep looking. The dog pulls harder. She looks at the dog, at the whip, at me. Hesitates. Then yells, "*Raus!* Get out you swine. You will be dead before I give you permission of any kind! *Niemals.* Never. *Raus!*"

I leave. Once outside I start trembling. Uncontrollably. I fear the dog, the whip, the rage. But in that place at that time I do look an SS in the eye. My fullest moment of freedom. Short lived, but full. She does not get my total subservience.

Why does my name enrage her so?

What about the name Judit enrages her?

Where did my courage come from?

Where did my courage come from? From the mud on her boots—a crack in the order? From her caring gesture of petting the dog? My fantasy perhaps of our commonality in appearance?

My anger at her insulting my mother's choice of this name? Anyu liked it, "A good name, Judit, of the Bible and of today." I too like the name. It is one of the few things about me I do not want to change. I ponder my reasons for courage. Does she question her reasons for hate? Those centuries of teaching, that old contempt intensified in this Heil universe.

The horror of it—a biblical name elicits murderous rage.

The horror of it—a young girl risks her life by merely looking at another female.

The horror of it—that I should see my behavior as an act of courage.

The horror of it—that she should see this act as criminal disobedience.

Stupid, stupid labels defining me, defining her. How boxed in we are. Still, I have less room to maneuver than she does.

It is April, the season of Passover—my exodus moment.

## Tell Your Father

Tell your Father
who art in Heaven
His will be done
and you want
your good name
your good
family name
cleared.
Loud and cleared

Granted. I have no claim
on you
but being of the same
family
a name

tarnished
reflects upon
  reflects upon
It's time
tell Him


   Tell Him also — not by bread alone, but without it?

**Songs.** After the evening soup, here, too, the women in their bunks discuss recipes—for nut cake, dumplings...

   Sometimes we sing. When even the recipe talk has been exhausted and there is energy, we sing. Someone starts, usually one of the two Polish sisters. They sing the Polish songs in lovely voices. Some of us know Yiddish songs and I also join in with the Czech, Slovak, and Hungarian singers. Off key, but I know the words. In this Siemens sub-camp nationalities are more mixed...Dutch, French, and Greek are here as well, and their songs.

   The German woman with a black triangle, "a-social," starts to sing a German song. *"Ach, du lieber Augustine."* No one joins in. There is silence and she stops. She nods her head and says *"Ich weiss."* She *weiss* German is not the language of song here. I feel closer to her—to her sadness.

   Women here were forced to sing German songs while marching to work in Auschwitz. In Ravensbrück, too, singing is often ordered, German singing.

   Blockälteste, do you cry during the Polish songs? She is usually in her own private room at this time of evening. I suspect she hears us and even though this singing is *verboten,* she allows it when it is safe. She is Polish.

   Song here is escape—momentary blocking of hunger and fear.

   Song here is remembrance—we were once of another world. We hear the echoes.

I place flowers of remembrance on Lake Schwedtsee for those whose ashes from the camp crematoria were dumped there, 1995. Photo by author.

World, in song too we remember you. How do you remember us? Do you sing lamentations for our absences? Are there dents where we were?

Singing is much less frequent than recipe talk.

From the Siemens camp you can see Lake Schwedtsee. The outside world is visible from here, not a brick wall but a high-voltage electric fence surrounds this camp. Calm waters with two swans, and on the banks, trees. A world out there—peaceful, natural. Real?

How can this be? The normal surprises me; the unimaginable is staring at me twenty-four hours a day.

(Later I learn that the ashes from the nearby crematoria were dumped into this lake. Later I place flowers onto the water—for those I knew and for those who have no one to place a flower for them.)

# Chapter Eight

## Leaving Camp

April, 1945. We expect the war to end. There are trees with leaves all around the camp. Women are in line—each carrying a basket. It is warm, not cold, not wet. No one is pushing. Horse drawn carriages drive by. The coachmen are men from my village—I recognize them. Each carriage stops at the front of the line and women get in.

"*Idete domu. President Roosevelt nás poslal.*" You are going home, the loudspeaker announces in Czech, President Roosevelt sent us.

I am moving closer to the front of the line. The woman next to me is pulling at my arm. "Didn't I tell you? Didn't I tell you? Roosevelt!"

Ella is shaking me. "Didn't I tell you to stay awake?! We are leaving the camp. They are evacuating us."

I had fallen asleep leaning against the wall. Last night we had been gathered into the main hall and told to await further orders. No one is to sleep in her bunk or leave the building for any reason. Personal belongings can be taken along. I have my bowl, spoon, and kerchief-sized towel. The red of my cotton polkadot dress is faded into yellow-pink, and the white dots reflect the colors of camp misery. The dress has never been washed in Ravensbrück. My brown sweater of Erika's procurement is fully stretched to serve as coat. When rain shrinks it, I stretch it again. Ella has her two rags—backup lining for her clogs.

We are marched into the main camp, the usual lineup of fives. The square is filled with women. I have never seen so many of us here.

I run off to say good buy to Erika. Though there are guards and dogs around, due to the large crowd it is not so hard to get away. Erika explains the whole camp is being evacuated. All must leave. Only the very sick will stay behind. She will stay to care for them.

"Soon you will see your father," she says. Always comforting.

End of April 1945. Rumors, the war is ending imminently. The end is here. We hug. The news gives hope and energy. For some the end comes before the end.

Ravensbrück is overcrowded. Prisoners arrive from Auschwitz and other camps in the East. They are the survivors of suffocating wagon trains and brutal marches.

Carts with the dead women are still full, fuller, as are the washroom floors. The more crowded the camp, the more crowded the washroom floor. More dead women in the bunks and larger piles of bodies in front of the blocks. Sometimes there is movement on the pile—a hand pushes out, or there is sound. No one checks, the living are not allowed to challenge Nazi death verdicts. But I hear of women who manage to crawl out and away before the cart arrives. The dead bodies are usually naked, their skin looks stretched and transparent, shroud-like.

There must be someone here who mourns someone here, but all I see is us stepping over women's bodies, not looking away. They are used to murdering and we are used to the murdered.

God?

⟡

### Death March

When unshod
a faster gait
prevents the feet
from sticking to
the ice and sleet

when shod in clogs
bruised and sored
a slower pace
is preferred

The Commandant
and his crew
with planned precision
knew
that either step
would do
to undo

**The march.** Our long line is stopped in front of the camp storage depot and each is given a Red Cross food package. How long have these packages been in storage? Available to them, but not to their intended recipients? Joy, in my hands food!

Guards, dogs, thousands of us and our Red Cross packages leave Ravensbrück. Where to? No official information is given.

Rumors: away from the enemy; we will be traded to the Americans for German war prisoners; we will be taken to the forest and shot; we will be enslaved in another camp. As always our certainties are speculations. We disregard their euphemistic facts... "East," "Safety," "*Planmässig zurückgezogen*," "Re-settlement," "*Arbeit macht frei.*"

But "evacuation" must mean something. What?

Dusk. On an open field we open our packages—cheese, crackers, chocolates, sardines. Food and time to eat it in. They allow us to drink from the small pond nearby. SS and dogs, but no walls, no barbed wire.

"Look at the trees," I tell Ella. "Look at all those trees."

No leaves yet, but there will be. We sleep outdoors without blankets and huddle for warmth. I sleep with the leftover food in my arms. Fullness in my hands.

Next day a new reality. Many are sick. Our digestive system is shrunk and cannot accommodate the rich and abundant food. We know death from starvation, but death from eating? Women are vomiting and many die that first day and after. At every stage death finds a way into our midst. When we starve, when we eat, when we are inside the camp, or outside it, when we attempt to escape the horror, when we attempt to stay with it.

Death? Are they forcing you into overtime?

Ella and I agree to ration our food more carefully. "We will do whatever is necessary," I state firmly. The trees here bring my Kurima plum trees closer. I must get there. Ella senses this and gently pats my head, which surprises me. Not her intuitiveness—her demonstrativeness. Not her style.

The lines of marchers are thinned daily. A woman has dysentery. She runs to the ditch and is shot. A woman slows down—the guard prods her with the rifle—she moves faster, then collapses. He shoots her.

In front of me Vera is supporting her mother, Shari. She practically carries her. Mother says, "I cannot go on."

Vera yells, "You must, you must!"

Mother falls and refuses to get up. The guard watches, comes over, kicks her. She does not rise. He shoots.

Vera cries, begs. *"Mir auch schiessen—mir auch. Ich mit Mutter."* She is Hungarian. Learns some German words in camp—To me, shoot also. To me also—I with mother. He grins and moves on.

God, does this not offend?

Ella and I take Vera by the arm and march on. Vera and her mother survive Auschwitz, Buchenwald, and Ravensbrück. Always together. Mother tells often how they defied Mengele in Auschwitz, where Vera pulls mother from the selection group—pulls her from left to right. She also rescues her from selections in Ravensbrück. Mother is badly beaten when she steals a turnip for Vera. They are seen by us as a model mother/daughter team. Now Vera wants to be dead with mother. We pull her along. Alone, the odds are bad.

On day two I still hear the shots. Then it becomes background noise. I no longer turn around. The bodies along the side of the road are not naked like in Ravensbrück, not eaten by rats, but dead like in Ravensbrück. If a prisoner dies during the night, her wearable shoes are quickly confiscated.

I am tired. My leftover food was dropped when helping Vera. Whatever is dropped cannot be retrieved. You would get trampled by the marching crowd. Every move, every step, every misstep has the potential for death.

Ella shares her remaining food with me and Vera, though Vera is not interested in food. We put cheese into her mouth, she chews but seems disconnected from herself, from her surroundings. Somehow she appears stronger, as though disconnecting from here gives her energy. Where is she? Will she collapse if she reconnects?

We have not been given additional food since leaving the camp.

I am tired. Vera is now walking on her own, unsupported by Ella and me. She still says nothing and moves on robot like. We do not comfort her, just keep her with us. I, too, move robot like—one leg ahead of the other, the other, the other, the other. . . . This is not spontaneous movement. It is movement I am directing with all my might. All my focus, all my being is in the legs—the rest of me—there is no rest of me. I am numbed out.

I ignore the shots. God, are they audible to you?

Ella and I try to stay close to each other with Vera between us. One small step backward or forward and we may never find each other on this march, even if we both stay alive.

### I say damn you

I say a corpse
I say a shooting
I say a dog
let loose
I say damn you
I say damn you
be damned I
say
because I say
a corpse a shooting
a dog let loose —
with ease

Will this daughter of Kurima lose all her capacity for compassion? God, let me not get used to everything.

Morning. Before we are marched out, three women are brought back to the group by guards and dogs. They tried to escape, are brought back to be shot in front of us. The guards are in a hurry— they do not take time to torture, just shoot. Perhaps some few do manage to escape into the forested area. Ella and I have a tentative plan. We do not talk about it anymore. Noach and Yossi, are you escaping?

Another night's sleep on an open field. I wake to a disturbing sight—Ella is still asleep. She is always up before me. Should I let her sleep? The awakening whip is coming toward us. I shake Ella, again, again, forcefully. She finally opens her eyes and sits up. Then she is finally awake. Awake, her determination reawakens. If left to sleep would she just sleep on forever? My ever-watchful Aunt Ella? I realize again her vulnerability is in what she cannot control. Is sleep taking over? From now on I must wake before her. I notice her skirt is so loose and flapping—it shifts further and further down from her waist; she has difficulty holding it up. Like the rest of us, Ella too is shrinking. There is so little left of her. Perhaps because of her resolute stance, I notice her diminution less.

"Take my rope," I offer, removing it from my waist. "My soup bowl is just useless weight anyhow. No need to carry it." I am now totally devoid of any possessions, but feel relieved about Ella's "holding it together."

The roads are crowded with Germans. Civilians pushing carts, bicycles, and baby carriages. Wounded soldiers in horse-drawn carriages and on foot. Soldiers retreating from the Russian front in stained uniforms and muddy boots. Bandaged limbs. The bandaged heads stand out. In the ditches dead horses with legs pointing to the sky. How sacrificial they look. I have seen dead women lying face up, but not horses. Tears come. I am less used to dead animals.

Trucks and tanks. Overhead planes.

Marching male slave laborers, brought into the Reich to work in factories and fields—"ethnics," brought here by force from occupied territories—they come onto this road from Labor rather than Concentration Camps. In ragged clothing but not as emaciated as we, they appear energized by this spectacle of defeat. Confident of their own survival and liberation they march briskly ahead of their guards.

Cannon shots behind us. Bombs nearby. Burning buildings. All movement is in one direction, to the West. Away from the Russians, *"An die Amerikaner."* They fear the enemy behind; we fear the enemy, the ever, always present enemy around us. It seems all the world's living and barely living, all the world's wounded and dead, are on this highway.

Thousands of people and hardly any human sounds. Rifle shots, cannon shots, planes, bombs, fire engines, motorcycles, trucks, they produce the sounds. Even the guards are silent, no *schnell*, no *Jude*, no *halt*, they just shoot wordlessly.

The empty bottle on the road is smashed by a bullet. A minute ago a civilian woman passes by with a girl. She hands one of our women prisoners the bottle with some liquid. The guard rushes over instantly, knocks the bottle out of the prisoner's hand, and shoots into the bottle. He does not look at either woman. Yes, he could have shot both. This human gesture by one woman to another justifies murder. Is the soldier finally tired of shooting into women? Is he preoccupied with his own survival? Is he saving a bullet knowing the prisoner will die of thirst anyway?

# Chapter Nine

# Liberation

We wake up on a field near a farmhouse. Two soldiers drag a man in civilian clothing behind the barn. He is shot in the head and falls. One soldier removes the watch from the dead hand. The soldiers are Russians. We are liberated. "*Ukrainsky*," explains the soldier with the watch, pointing to the dead man. Liberation. The SS are gone. The dogs are gone. Different uniforms, different armies. Same shots. I hate the world!

Yesterday I am immune to the murder of women. Today I despair at the shooting of the enemy. But I had such other visions of liberation. Embraces and warm bread, flowers even. A welcoming celebration—us and the liberators. Us, the focus, not some scared *Ukrainsky*. I do not know if this man is guilty or not. The Ukrainians often outdid the Nazis in their brutality. They hate the Russians full force and the Jews even more. But now I want scenes to look at, not avert my eyes from. Life I want, loveliness, not death.

Soon I focus on loveliness.

Liberation is women, yesterday's prisoners, washing potatoes by the pump preparing our first meal of freedom. Washing. Potatoes.

Liberation is sitting on a chair.

Liberation is messing around with the door, open—close—open.

Drinking from a cup

Women greeting men—inviting newly arriving men in prison stripes—for stew and apples.

A Russian soldier comes into the yard carrying loaves of bread. He hands them to me. I say, *"Spaziba,"* thank you, taught to me in the TB ward by Marina, my Russian prisoner-of-war friend. She also taught me a Russian folk song, *Katyusha*, a favorite of the soldiers. I sing it. The soldier joins in, laughs, and kisses me. Nice. Liberation is good.

## Liberation

The trees are
growing leaves,
I said, "Lucky trees
we do not have to
eat your leaves"

"Cat," I said
"do not strut,
like you, I too can
come and go
without
accountability"

"God," I said
"I will not
sacrifice,
but come and
share
our new baked bread"

Perhaps he too is hungry for bread and for live humans.

**Shoes for Ella.** Inside the empty farmhouse Ella looks for shoes. She finds a man's pair. She also finds three pairs of socks. Although it is May and quite mild, she puts on all the socks, one on top of the other. She says, "I will never have cold feet again." Considers saving her wooden clogs "to remember."

By now the clogs have no soles left, only wooden sides. Ella holds them up, then laughs, "Every cell of my every toe will remember. I should pray to forget!" The clogs with no soles are left behind. I tell her, "From now on clogs only on picture postcards."

In the mirror of the old hotel in the nearby town I see myself. I look younger and older. Underdeveloped and ancient. Everyone approaches the mirror with hesitancy. Helena stands there with one eye open. She slowly opens the other eye and yells: "*Én vagyok, it vagyok!*" I am. I am here! Berta looks in the mirror and cries. After the head shaves in Ravensbrück, people do not recognize others—now it is their own appearance they have to reclaim.

I wash my hair. Then I find scissors and cut it. My freedom time act of defiance. I do not want their gift of my uncut hair. Now I feel liberated. Exhilarated. Self liberated. Ella celebrates her shod feet, and I, my scalped head.

### Death, stand aside at my liberation time

Death stand aside
do not hover by
my side!
watch, I leap
I touch the sun
push children's swings

stop motor cars
wear sandals that
are open-toed.
I run, I hum
am everywhere.
Don't mess with me
you bloated creep
you cannot
run as fast
as me

My unrestricted body celebrates!

Prisoners arrive from other camps. Lists of survivors are posted in various places. I am not ready to check; the lists don't list absences, these are registered on the faces of the searchers. "Come back tomorrow, we will have new lists," say the officials. For some tomorrow is a good day. I am not checking.

In Ravensbrück hopes of family returns were more concrete, more insistent, needed survivor bricks. My expectations now are more vulnerable. Less certain. I am not checking.

I bathe, I eat, wear clean underwear, talk to people who do not talk of camp only. Short hand, okay. No details.

Judith: "You?"

Sam: "Auschwitz," shows me his tattoo.

Judith: "Bad—eh?"

Sam: "You?"

Judith: "Ravensbrück."

Sam: "Not so good."

There are some who talk of nothing else, nothing, nothing else. For now, of nothing else. Others are silent, outwardly. Will the rest of our lives always echo these sounds and visions? Outwardly? Inwardly?

**Reunion.** Ella, where is Ella? Find her. Quickly. My aunt is found. Noach and Yossi, her husband and son, stand in the doorway of this inn somewhere in Germany. We are reunited—four who entered Ravensbrück—still four. A record.

Noach, always slender, is more recognizable. His shaved head is growing whiteness. Yossi looks more like Noach—his father—than Noach does. Gaunt, aged, muscleless. In the striped prisoner pants and German officer's coat he is both the vanquished and the victor. In Yossi's case the stripes survived—the officer?

We head towards home.

## A brief reprieve

I do not wish to forget, just
a brief reprieve
to remember
seasonal shoes
open-toed or snow resistant
a lunch table with rolls
left over
a muscled father in charge
comforting
a scraped knee (humorously)
a laughing dog
Shabbath candles
gray hair

I wish to remember
the place, before,
before, the after overlay.

Good thoughts for a while
before I die

**Going home.** "They are coming back after all," says the woman to her companion in the front seat of the carriage. "Who, who came back?" I shout. She does not answer. This last leg of the journey home is by horse-drawn carriage. Transportation is either non-existent, erratic, or unreliable. It has taken months to get here from Germany—by bus, train, buggies, and walking and walking. Back in Kurima, they are surprised, less at my scrawny appearance than that I appear at all.

Kurima. How can so little, so nothing, be changed? Houses are intact. Painted mustard yellow, blue, orange. Roses and chickens. The language is the same Slovak without the shrieking German intrusions. The storks are back on the parish-house chimney, secure in their belongingness from spring to autumn. Vegetable shoots are pushing up through Omama's garden soil. I check the plum trees. Small fruit is already forming.

I recognize Mrs. Altman's tablecloth on the clothesline, hung there by a young pregnant woman. She is not Mrs. Altman.

Kurima seen from Ravensbrück is whole and home. Kurima from back here is indecent in its wholeness—it should look scarred and shattered. The intact houses are like gaping holes with the missing. Missing. Missing. Missing. Where are signs of the wounds, some markers of the missing? Missing, Mr. Treitel from the bicycle shop. The rabbi's wife on the front porch rocking her baby son. The rabbi. Hershi, looking for his big brother, Baruch. Evka, waiting for that letter from America. Missing Karpu, Yidu, Irenke. My anyu.

a sated body and no lice
do not suffice
once you survive,
I am glad of that
in there I thought

such state
to be
the kindest fate

Our Kurima family has the largest number of survivors, cousins Elza, Mella, and my Mirjam come back from hiding, I from Ravensbrück. Mrs. Rappaport returns alone, David Altman alone, Blanca alone, Baruch, Edith, alone. No one else. Not one intact family returns. We four girls wait for our fathers to return. They do not.

Our fathers, the brothers, Moshe and Ele, are born in the same house. They marry on the same day, live in the same residence, share business and fields. Together they slave in the Slovak Labor Camp. Escape together, hide, are caught together. In Sachsenhausen they both hold out until—Moshe dies a few days before liberation, Ele dies shortly after the Red Army enters the camp.

Dare no one say—They Did Not Resist.

After a while no Jew stays on in Kurima. This unchanged place does not fit.

**Great Britain.** The British Government invites 1,500 child and teen survivors into Britain. Only half that number can be found. An army bomber is our wings from that gaping, empty place. My first plane ride. First sight of an ocean. We sing out of joy and anxiety. The journey is again uncertain, but of hope, not terror.

Mirjam is nine; we will not be separated so I go with her to Weir Courtney, a beautiful children's home in the country. Here now are the children who survived Auschwitz, Theresienstadt, Buchenwald. The youngest group, age three to five, come to Theresienstadt as infants. Here are also children known as

"Mengele's twins" from Auschwitz, ages five, six, and seven. They were selected and kept alive by Mengele for his medical experiments. Experiments designed to provide "scientific data" on how to improve fertility rates for German women and to insure blue-eyed babies.

Alice Goldberger, the supervisor of the home and herself a refugee from Berlin, writes monthly reports on the children.

## QUOTES FROM ALICE'S REPORTS

Vicky, 6: "Do soldiers shoot God?"

Gadi, 5: "I want a puppy that's frightfully frightened of me."

Denny, 6: "I was quite bent and crooked when I came out—she did this with the other children as well." Referring to being locked in a closet in Theresienstadt. Possibly hidden to avoid deportation to Auschwitz.

Gadi, 5: "God sits on the roof and puts all the people in prison."

Mirjam, 9: "It is much nicer to die in peacetime."

Julius, 8: "But who deaded him?" referring to a person who died in a car accident. Julius cannot conceive of death other than by Nazis.

Sylvia, 8: "Are those children you were with all dead now?" Alice answers, "No."

Sylvia: "Then why did you go away from them?" She knows only one reason for separation—death.

Berli, 5: The children refuse to eat lettuce. "We already had to eat grass when we had nothing else. We don't like it anymore."

Denny, 5: "I am lucky that I was not killed when I was a baby so I could get this tricycle."

Renate, 15: "I never thought I could listen to birds or see a tree again. I only wanted to come out and kill all the Germans. But now I am so glad if I look out of the window and see birds and grass."

Vicki, 6: Touching the walls of the house, "When will this house go away again? How long can we stay?"

Berli, 5: "Look, such lovely bath, warm water, not cold only."

Judith: "Look, such lovely shower—it gives water," say I soundlessly. That other place sticks to us.

# Chapter Ten

# After

Yes, to this day I am affected by the Holocaust. I have been fortunate and have had a good, full life since those times. Family, friends, education, work, fun. I also live on two tracks—always. I am here and I am there, when I have a shower, when I eat potatoes, when I am hungry, when I am not. When I sneeze I think in hiding that would be a give away. If an infant cries, will there be milk? Water? A mother? I do not wear striped clothing. I own sturdy boots. I do not turn off bad news on TV; the bad news should be heard by someone. In supermarkets I do not select fruits or vegetables. I just take those from the top. I cannot engage in "selections" because of Auschwitz—because of Mengele.

I assess all people—would this person have survived? Would she share a potato? Would she know how to steal one? Would we kill lice together?

I assess all Christian people—would this person hide me?

In parenting I deliberately provide for good moments, for warmth in harsh times. I try to engage in *Tikun Olam*, the repair of the world. And when the time comes I want an un-Auschwitz funeral.

## You Are Invited To My Funeral

You are invited
to my funeral
to my un-Auschwitz funeral.
Attire optional —
no stripes please.
Come nearer,
come nearer
and attest
that beneath this poplar tree
this season-marking-poplar-tree
in this pleasant ground
chosen and paid for —
with space reserved nearby
for husband to join
in timely manner
for company and closeness —
attest people,
that Yehudit
the person Yehudit
Yehudit the Jew
is according to custom
here buried.
You come too, Lord.
(were you too embarrassed to
attend in Auschwitz?)
You come too, Lord
and smile —
Your will be done.
No! Not smile!
Just be

There is a cemetery on a hill with poplar trees and a view, where Reuven and I own twelve burial plots, reserved just for the two of us. Ground and space and concreteness.

## FOLLOW-UPS

**Aunt Ella.** Feet first. Immediately after liberation my aunt attends to her feet. She finds and wears three pairs of socks and man's shoes—leather. And while the rest of us relish bread and potatoes, Ella acquires asparagus from a German farm. Asparagus. Classiness comes naturally. Becomes her. After her husband, Noach, dies, she escapes the Russian occupation of Czechoslovakia and lives in a Displaced Person's Camp in Germany, where she eventually settles. Later, when I plan to visit her with my family, she sends me three letters requesting information of our favorite foods. I choose asparagus to please her and poppy seed cake to please me.

**Our friends.** The brothers Baruch and Hershi are sent to Auschwitz. Hershi is killed; Baruch survives and settles in Israel. He becomes Kurima's memory. Sees to it that Kurima is recorded at Yad Vashem, the Holocaust Memorial Museum in Jesusalem. He is in touch with the mayor of Kurima and arranges for the maintenance of the Jewish cemetery.

**Regina.** Listen, God, to Regina's story. A sad, bad story it is. In Ravensbrück Regina is separated from her husband and son. Sam is eleven. Soon husband and son are sent to another camp where husband dies. When the camp is liberated by Americans, an American soldier befriends Sam, wants to take him to America and adopt him. UNRA, the United Nations Relief Association, is contacted by Regina, who survives and is searching for her family. People are urging her to give her son to the soldier "His life will be so much better in America." Regina loses one child to the oppressors and is now to lose another to the rescuers? Should she have to consider such an option?

For such choices is she liberated? A curse upon the pain of her mothering.

God, have you heard them all? All the stories? Too many?

**Erika.** In Revier—TB Block 10, Erika shares her crackers with me, adding life to my emaciated body. Keeps an eye on me. Keeps me alive with an added potato. Discharges me to avoid selection. She smiles at me, cares, hopes.

I want to connect with her. My attempts to contact her after the war prove unsuccessful. In 1995, during my visit to Ravensbrück, I tell the gathering of my gratitude to Erika. A young German woman approaches me. "My name is Grit Weichelt. I have written a biography of Erika Buchmann. Would you like to read it?" She sends me the book to America. I read Erika's commitment to remember. "We who per chance remained alive will work incessantly as living witnesses of your wretched lives and deaths. We feel deeply the responsibility to safeguard your memory."

I read that on April 28, 1945, she too had to leave camp and go on the death march. She leaves with the last group. Due to the chaotic situation on the road, she, together with two friends, manages to escape and hide in the nearby forest. They are liberated by the Russian Army two days later. Erika returns to Ravensbrück to care for the sick. Five hundred tubercular patients are miraculously abandoned by the SS.

The Red Army forces over five hundred inhabitants from the nearby town of Furstenberg to help clean up conditions in the camp. For many patients help comes too late. Erika remains there until the end of June, making sure appropriate arrangements are made for the surviving prisoners. Only then does she return to her family in Stuttgart, where she is joined by her newly liberated husband from Sachsenhausen. Her second daughter is born in 1947. The women in Erika's circle in Ravensbrück make a pledge that if they survive they will bring children into this world—a reaffirmation of life. Erika is forty-five years old when her second daughter is born.

Erika becomes active in the establishment of the National Memorial and Museum of Ravensbrück. She also experiences more sorrow—her younger daughter commits suicide. Erika died of cancer in November 1971.

**Cheesecake.** I enter a bakery in Prague. Hanicka, from my Ravensbrück bunk, is in there buying cheesecake. The chestnut colored hair reaches down to her waist. I last see her with a scalped head. Will she not cut her hair again? After a strong, happy hug, I exclaim, "I heard you bake a hundred cheese cakes in Ravensbrück! Those perfect recipes! None better, you claimed."

She nods. "That was my husband's favorite. Stefan did not come back."

Hanicka is remarried. She buys ready-made cheesecake.

**Frieda's family.** From hiding place to hiding place. Caught and sent to Auschwitz. By successfully escaping into Czechoslovakia they avoid the earlier Hungarian deportations—postpone Auschwitz. Any less time spent in Auschwitz.... But Uncle Laci dies there. Frieda and her children, Trudi and Nisu, survive. I suspect their Auschwitz experience was worse than my Ravensbrück one. We do not talk about either.

**Apu.** Shortly after our marriage and arrival in America, Reuven and I are invited to a wedding. I sit next to a man and when I tell him I am from Kurima, he exclaims, "I know you—I was with your father in Sachsenhausen. He always spoke of the family, Friday evening meals and *zmirot*, Sabbath hymns. I even know where at table you sat." My father was in Sachsenhausen, one half hour from Ravensbrück. We did, of course, not know of each other's presence. At this time of hunger we connected through family food—thirty kilometers and forever apart.

God, we knew you well in Kurima. Where we were, you were. Like breathing. And there, in there, were those sights unfit for Godly eyes?

## If God Is Dead

If God is dead
where is he dead
above which Auschwitz sky?
At rest perhaps in garden's shade
in empty Eden's grace?
Where do we light the candle
if God is dead?
If God is dead
we must not leave him
unattended —
nor us
   nor us

Not dead, not dead. Please not dead. Accountable.

## Are things changed in heaven?

Would You come down
that ladder — that ladder
Jacob climbed?
I will not deal with angels
I'll wait till You arrive.

Granted. Your Job directed reprimand
is well crafted
and of high design

What do You tell them
the Auschwitz them?

when last seen
shoeless and selected

What say You to the killers
and those who know not
— know not?

By what name do we call You ?
are things changed in heaven
as they are on earth?

When You come down
that ladder — that ladder
Jacob climbed,
I'll hold on tight
for answers
    and for You

What say You to them? The gypsy child, the crazed mother, the German nun, Russian warrior, Dutch resister, Czech physician. The Jewish bride, the Jewish sister, teacher, dressmaker, grandmother, aunt, the Jewish everyone.

I would so like to know. Were you lonely in those empty Synagogues? Sat you in that empty Eden again? Our Godly connections were severed. No Shabbat candles. No prayer books. No rabbi, no Torah. No bread to be blessed. No Bar Mitzvah. No Exodus celebration. We kept the Day-of-Fast. Kept it into days, weeks, last days.

Our connections severed. Yours?

Who should apologize for my blasphemy?

I grow flowers. God, in my garden I have no quarrel with You. There, I awe. There I say, Amen.

## That chair out there

That chair out there
I do not share, mine
it is,
this earned bliss

Iron wrought, grandiose,
a seat to watch my garden
strut and swing, exuberate,
celebrate

My garden knows, when,
what color, how.
but did I not lend
a hand?
mix up the green,
juxtapose yellow, pink,
deep lavender?

Sit next to me
silently.
I hear you whisper, "nice, so
pleasing to the eyes"

But, I tell you this,
for soul to taste the soil,
for bliss like this, you must
a touch of genesis

Indelible memories demand their presence.

## Summer Woods

This late year
I would like to see
a summer wood
and not worry
is it deep enough
dense enough
to hide me?

This late year
I say
it is now far enough
late enough
to live here now,
   so let the shower be just that
   and the railway tracks
   potatoes too, see they are plentiful.
But how do you disconnect
from Lager Ravensbrück?

I am old in this late year
but my soul — my soul
is peopled with parents
who are younger than my children.
My brother will forever be eight.

I wish for a cemetery with gravestones
with the name of, with the name of,
with the name of,
Lord, it would help
if you would light some candles
say Kaddish —

they would appreciate that
me too
You too, perhaps?

I will also plant a garden
this late year
and visit Barcelona and Jerusalem,
swim with grandchildren.
Survivorship territory
multiple residences
lived in simultaneously —
this place / that other place.

World, I have a question
world of ethnic cleansing —
who is clean?

This late year
I wish for us to see
the Summer Woods.

## INTRUSIONS INTO THE FUTURE

**Triggers.** Living in London. Studying Social Work at the London School of Economics. I take the Underground (subway) and get off at Holborn Station. There are several exits and I am confused as to which is right. I ask the policeman near the central ticket booth, "Which way to L.S.E.?"

Every morning, every school day, every year, "Which way—?" The different policemen on duty expect my question and, smiling, point the direction. Do they think I am flirting? Think me senile? They show no irritation and continue to help.

Postcard to myself from Ravensbrück on the fiftieth anniversary of liberation,1995. Courtesy of author.

I do genuinely have a poor sense of direction—my dreams are filled with not finding my way. However, I do feel satisfaction in being able to spunkily approach a uniformed authority without fear. And be helped.

**Triggers.** Our son Allen is born. I have a breast infection and cannot continue to nurse him. The doctor has never seen such a panic stricken, enraged, hysterical woman. "Calm down. Your son will have a bottle, he will be fine." How does he not understand that a mother cannot depend on that bottle—cannot count on that milk. Allen thrives on the bottle. I do not explain to the doctor my outburst. He would find me an unfit mother.

**Triggers.** Son David is at the university. He very much wants a hi-fi set to study by. An expense we cannot afford at this time.

I say to Reuven, "Let's get it for him."

To me I say, "Let David have music inside him, for the trenches, for hard times." Survivor building bricks.

**Triggers.** I take a five-hour train ride to lunch with Allen between his college classes. Memory building.

**Triggers.** April, 1995. My comments in the Guest Book at the Ravensbrück Museum—formerly SS Headquarters:

> "Fifty years ago I come her involuntarily—a Jewish girl from Slovakia. Now I am here at the invitation of the German Government and most welcomed by our German hosts. Your program logo of "**95–45**" is complex for us survivors, because the 45 is not as faded in our lives as your logo implies. We still live on two tracks—the past and the now. I have great curiosity to know how the SS and their supporters integrate their experiences. Do they too have nightmares? Remorse? Our legacy is involuntarily passed on to our children. What of their children? What do their children do with their legacy?"
>
> — Judith Sherman, April 26, 1995

**Triggers.** 1995, Ravensbrück. A survivor from Poland sits in front of me during the Commemoration Ceremony of the fiftieth anniversary of the liberation. Her umbrella is opened for shade, blocking my view of the speakers' platform. Requests to close the umbrella are ignored. I know I can insist and can even get help from the uniformed guides nearby.

Options for choice. Opportunities for improvement. Uniformed help. In Ravensbrück?

I do nothing. I decide to let the woman have a moment of victory in Ravensbrück. A moment of victory for us both. She has comfort and I have options. In Ravensbrück.

**Triggers.** Over a half-century later. "*Ha ben sheli*—that is my son being Bar Mitzvat." The beaming woman in the red straw hat at the Western Wall in Jerusalem is offering me poppy-seed cake from the large platter she is carrying. She does not know me, but includes me in her celebration. I take the cake. I cry. I am back in the Gestapo prison where the guards feast on poppy-seed cake, and I crave some discomfort on their part for ignoring my presence.

Keep your cake but acknowledge me! Now I cry. A full moment in Jerusalem. Tears well saved.

**Triggers.** 9/11/2001. The Terror of Tuesday scratches images onto all our souls and minds. And the connections. I am thinking of the Holocaust survivors who, after liberation, go from the world of terror to the world of chaos and hope—with names, with names—looking for loved ones. Now I have a new "forever" image. I see on television a young girl, in sneakers, jeans, hair tied back. In her hand a photograph, "Have you seen my dad?"

### Has Anybody Seen My Dad?

Has any body seen my dad?
his name is Arnie —
Arnie...is my dad.
He wears a tie
that's purple — pink
the one that I
have given him.

Oh, you'd recognize my dad
between his front teeth
there is a gap,
probably the reason why
on this photograph
he does not smile.

Did you see my dad?
My dad called home
on the cell-phone
told my mom
"there is a fire
and I cannot see —

I love you Ellie
and tell the kids
I…"

Have you seen my dad?
The hospitals say
"No, not yet,
not yet, not yet."

You call if you see my dad,
and I'll keep looking for you, Dad.
Please God, oh, God
where is my dad?
Where — is — my — dad?

Her life will go on and she will keep looking

How do they deal with their past? What do they tell their children?

## We should talk

We should talk.
This half century later
we should talk
Two grandmothers we should talk

I cannot bear
to wear
stripes.
Your swastika
safely sheltered in
family Bible

tissue wrapped, is it?
Your glory days

That blue-gray coat
high polished boots
seen by downcast
untermensch eyes
(blue like yours)
I remember
Your glory days

Your dog so helpful
so obedient
so well trained
(they don't make them
like that anymore).
Me a blur or less in
that messy field of
thousand thousand blurs?
Your vision clear
— Judenrein

Is today, today for you?
Is there a doubt,
a stain, a child directed
hesitation?
We should talk
Should — we — talk?

℃

A small stone is placed on the gravestone before Rosh Hashanah,
the New Year, for remembrance of loved ones. Invisible cemeteries hold my large collection of unplaced stones. And I also

carry their imprints, their legacies—joy, work, plum trees, love, awe, song.

A life of connections. A family of caring, tradition, aspiration leaves imprints. That place of terror leaves its branding. England opens its door—not soon enough, not wide enough. But in the spring of 1945 England shares its food rations, restructures our messed up lives with friendship, education opportunity. The green of England is the absolute green against which all other greens are measured.

In the Judean Hills, near Jerusalem, I meet Reuven—the American intrigued by life, matched by zest, eager to see every side of every mountain.

My gift to him

> she puts a smile
> upon his face
> — how rich both

and the demand that he stand up to me.

His gift to me

> let's walk
> and leave time
> for big cupped
> coffee

and a promise to type, but not correct my poems

Our strongest connections are now in America. With amazement and gratitude, I marvel at the ease of my children's Jewishness. Their mantle of Jew "so light, so safe, so *kol b'seder*."

Grandchildren attend shabbath services and soccer practice.

Connections—the essence of my work in Social Work. Connections—friendships, God, and garden.

### Fresh washed sheets

I am in love with
fresh washed sheets
my flower beds
the coffee shop
at every stop;
I love the zest of my love's quest
the spunk of grandchild
when sent to bed;
the pink stone of Jerusalem
the pleasing sound
Je-ru-sa-lem,
my hair when wet
from morning rain
a friend who says
let's lunch again,
a daughter's new maturity
in styling herself after me,
I am in love with
"enough for now"
I am in love with
"I want more"
I am in love with
fresh washed sheets
and purple-red anemones.

I do not discuss the Holocaust with my grandchildren. When my daughter Ora goes for a parent-teacher conference, she sees her daughter Ilana's poem hanging on the classroom wall. Ora had never seen the poem before. Family tradition—we each deal with this topic in our own way. My granddaughter Ilana is seven and a half at the time.

## This Very Bad News

One very nice day this horrible news spread through the town,
   the city, the state, the country and the continent.
This very bad news spread throughout the world.
The Jews set off hiding.
Were they scared? Did they chatter? Were they cold?
How many worries filled their head?
The bumpy, rocky forest.
Things to trip on. Branches to break.
Splinters to wait for.
Broken body parts indeed.
Some Christians set off for war. Other Christians hid Jews.
But some Christians just sat there.
But now things are calmer. No more worries to worry and no
   more fears to fear.
Now it is all peace and everyone glad.

But how scarred was she?
I wonder how long she had to hide?
I bet grandma felt sad when she found out that her mom, dad and
   brother died.
Where did the Nazis find her?
I'm even scared when I think about her life.
I know there were a lot of rocks, sticks, and stones, stumps to trip
   on and make noise with.
Millions of Nazis to watch out for.
So little ditches and secret hiding places, guns and bombs.
The noise of Nazi cars, bullets being blasted, bombs and shouting.

The wind blowing hard and making you chatter, worries in
   your head,
Three hours of sleep, wild animals to fight.
How scarred was she?

— Ilana Gelb

Age 7 1/2

A quote from my daughter Ora:

"We know that our parent's trauma did not end with liberation.
There were lifelong losses and adaptations to be made. I cannot
really comprehend how our parents rebuilt their lives. This to me
is the miracle. They formed relationships, had children, developed
careers, loved, and laughed. We witnessed and learned their
strength, resilience, and passion for life in addition to the sadness.
The group that suffered greatest evil known to mankind has been
able to impart values of kindness and morality to their children."

Children are born. David, Allen, Ora.
They bring Gina and Eric into the family.
Grandchildren are born. Ariel, Ilana, Aaron, Sara, Michael.
Joshua is the son of Mirjam.
Children and grandchildren, you have names of murdered
grandparents, gassed aunts and uncles.
You have names of those who carried little ones across the
brook. Planted corn, fixed roofs, lit lamps, swam in rivers, lit can-
dles. Made bread, made wine, danced and teased, drank buttermilk.
People of life. People of life. People of life... of life. People of life.

## <u>Survivor's Legacy Wish to Her Children</u>

Bread, always bread
stars that lighten the heavens
not brand your chests
always, always — water
trains to journeys of delight
with seats, windows,
tickets of return
no accent;
fathers to hold your children's hand
children who outgrow their shoes
Your mantle of "Jew"
of cloth so light
so safe
so Kol B"Seder;
mothers — oh yes — mothers —
mothers you can stand up to!
Israel to fill your soul.

and what of Auschwitz memory?
that too is in your legacy.